Clownfishes

IN THE AQUARIUM

T.F.H. Publications, Inc.
One TFH Plaza
Third and Union Avenues
Neptune City, NJ 07753

This book has been published with the intent to provide accurate and authoritative information in regard to the subject matter within. While every precaution has been taken in preparation of this book, the publisher and author assume no responsibility for errors or omissions. Neither is any liability assumed for damages resulting from the use of the information herein.

Library of Congress Cataloging-in-Publication Data
Skomal, Gregory B.
Clownfishes in The Aquarium / Gregory B. Skomal
p. cm.
Includes index.
ISBN 0-7938-0547-3 (alk. paper)
1. Anemonefishes. 2. Aquariums. I. Title.   -
SF458.A45S56 2004
639.3'772–dc22
2003027772

Front Cover Photo: Mark Smith
Back Cover Photos(l-r): Mark Smith, U.E. Friese, O. Lucanus

Book design by Mary Ann Mahon Kahn.

www.tfh.com

Clownfishes

IN THE AQUARIUM

Gregory B. Skomal

Table of Contents

Part Three: Caring for Your Clownfish

Part Four: Feeling Under the Weather

Part Five: Advanced Clown Keeping

Introduction

They say that when times are down, send in the clowns. I can't agree more, but you don't have to wait until times are down to bring home a clown—clownfish, that is! I can think of no group of fishes that I personally enjoy more than the beautiful, playful, and entertaining clownfishes. Colorfully painted, decorated like clowns, and equally as entertaining, these fishes are well named.

As an experienced marine biologist, I've had the wonderful opportunity to observe these fascinating fishes in their natural environment—on Pacific coral reefs. They are relatively small when compared to the thousands of species in these tropical ecosystems. Their fins are used primarily to hover and flutter, so they are also poor swimmers, unable to elude most predators when pursued. How, then, do these brightly colored, clumsy fishes thrive so well in places where predators loom around every corner? Their advantage lies in their choice of roommates—the deadly anemone, an invertebrate species with stinging tentacles and an appetite for fishes. The clownfishes are special, though. They can live and thrive among the stinging tentacles of the anemone, a lifestyle that gives them the more formal name of

anemonefishes. In the wild, the clownfishes rarely venture far from their protective home except to warily feed on a passing meal.

Life for the clownfishes is very different in the home aquarium, and they are indeed the ideal fish for the beginner. Clownfishes are hardy and tolerant of less than perfect aquarium conditions. They readily feed in captivity, and they don't need a lot of space because they are used to living in an anemone, which is small to begin with. But wait, there's more. In the wild, anemonefishes need anemones, but in the aquarium, they don't; the option is yours. Clownfishes are smart, capable of responding to humans, and entertaining to those that feed them. As an added bonus, clownfishes are among a handful of saltwater fishes that breed in captivity. This is particularly important for a number of reasons. First, your clownfishes were born and raised in captivity, so they are used to aquarium conditions, unlike other fishes that may have been captured from the wild and therefore have to adapt to life in a glass box. Secondly, they are healthier than most other fishes because they were exposed to less stress and did not have to endure capture and transport from the other side of the world. Third, clownfishes raised in captivity will help to preserve those that live in the wild, thereby having less impact on the world's fragile coral reef ecosystems. Finally, if you are so inclined, clownfishes may actually breed in your aquarium and you can raise your own little clowns.

With all these wonderful attributes, the clownfishes are surely destined to be part of your saltwater aquarium. So, whether you are building your watery circus from scratch, converting your freshwater aquarium, or simply adding clownfishes to your existing saltwater aquarium, this is your personal guide to accomplishing your goals—the right way!

Part One

Understanding Clownfishes

Chapter 1

Natural History
of Clownfishes

What are the Clownfishes?

There are over 20,000 kinds of fish in the world, and
about 11,000 live in saltwater. Like all living things, similar
kinds of fish have been grouped together into families. Each
"kind" of fish is commonly referred to as a species. Similar
species are grouped together into something called a genus.
Thus, every living thing, including clownfishes, has a first
name (the genus), and a last name (the species), much like
you and me. The genus is always capitalized and the species
is not, but both names are always underlined or italicized
(i.e. the percula clownfish, *Amphiprion percula*). Since
people speak many languages, it was decided centuries ago
that all these names would be written in Latin so that people
all over the world could use the same Latin or "scientific"
name to refer to that species.

What does this have to do with clownfishes? Simple, all
the clownfishes, also called anemonefishes, belong to a
family called Pomacentridae, which comprises 28 genera
(plural of genus) and includes over 320 species of small
tropical fishes. There are 28 species of clownfishes, and most
(27) of these are so similar that they have been placed into

a genus called *Amphiprion*, which is their first name. So, for example, the Percula Clownfish is called *Amphiprion percula*, and the Tomato Clownfish is called *Amphiprion frenatus*. The Maroon Clownfish is the only species that does not belong to the genus *Amphiprion*; its name is *Premnas biaculeatus*.

Now that I have thoroughly confused you, I'm not finished. Similar clownfish species have been broadly grouped into complexes. There are six complexes of clownfishes: The Percula Complex (2 species), the Tomato Complex (5 species), the Clarkii Complex (11 species), the Skunk Complex (6 species), the Saddleback Complex (3 species), and the Maroon Complex (1 species). Unfortunately, pet stores usually do not use scientific names; they use common names, which sometimes refer to more than one species. For example, the Ocellaris Clownfish has been marketed as the Percula Clownfish for a higher price. In addition, not all clownfish species are available to the average aquarist, but dealers will market other clowns under their name. A good example of this is the Sebae Clownfish, which is actually very rare, but that common name is incorrectly used for other species very frequently.

Bottom line: There are 28 species of clownfishes, and many of them are available to you at your pet dealer. However, not all clownfishes are ideal for the aquarium, let alone the beginner, so you have to choose your clownfish carefully. The following is a guide to all the clownfish species, with some recommendations about the ones that may be right for you.

These three-banded clownfish (Amphiprion tricinctus) *are living among the tentacles of their host anemone* (Heteractis aurora).

The Percula Complex

Ocellaris or False Percula Clownfish, *Amphiprion ocellaris*
This is the most common clownfish in the aquarium trade, with its distinctive mandarin color and three white bands bordered in black. This is the best clownfish for the beginner because it is hardy and mild-mannered. It grows to about 3 inches and will get along with others of the same kind.

The false percula clownfish (Amphiprion ocellaris) *is perhaps the most popular clownfish species available to marine hobbyists.*

Percula Clownfish, *Amphiprion percula*
This clownfish is remarkably similar to the Ocellaris, and sometimes the smaller specimens are difficult to tell apart. Perculas tend to have thicker black borders on their white bands, but this is not always the case. This is the smallest clownfish, only growing to about 2.5 inches. This is not the ideal clownfish for the beginner because the Percula is more expensive (at least twice the cost of an Ocellaris), requires better water quality, and tends to bully other clownfish and tankmates.

Percula clowns (Amphiprion percula) *are a smaller but more aggressive species of clownfish.*

The Tomato Complex

Tomato Clownfish, *Amphiprion frenatus*
Red and Black Clownfish, *Amphiprion melanopus*
All the clowns in the tomato complex have deeper bodies that are generally oval. Juveniles of the Tomato Complex have three stripes, but adults typically have only one white headband. The Tomato Clownfish ranges in color from orange to red and grows to over 4 inches. The Red and Black Clownfish is similarly colored and reached 3.5 inches, but its anal and pelvic fins are usually black, not red like the

Tomato Clown. These two species are great for the beginner because they are readily available and extremely hardy; they are also easy to breed in captivity.

Tomato clowns (Amphiprion frenatus) *grow quite large compared to many other species of clownfish.*

Red Saddleback Clownfish, *Amphiprion ephippium*
Australian Clownfish, *Amphiprion rubrocinctus*
McCulloch's Clownfish, *Amphiprion mccullochi*
These three very similar species of clownfish in the Tomato Complex are less common in the aquarium trade than the two previous species. Although the Red Saddleback Clownfish has a similar body shape to the others, the adult usually lacks the characteristic headband. This bright orange fish is hardy and good for the beginner, but it is intolerant of copper, which is typically used to treat aquarium protozoan diseases. The Australian Clownfish is a colorful burnt orange with a white headband, but it is a sensitive fish and not well suited for the beginner. McCulloch's Clownfish is a rare species that is dark brown or black with a white face and tail; it is not typically seen in the aquarium trade.

The red saddleback clownfish (Amphiprion ephippium) *is one of the most beautiful and desirable species available.*

The Skunk Complex
Skunk Clownfish, *Amphiprion akallopisos*
Pink Skunk Clownfish, *Amphiprion perideraion*
Orange Skunk Clownfish, *Amphiprion sandaracinos*
The three species of skunk clownfish are so named because of the white stripe that runs along the back, from the tip of the nose to the base of the tail. Don't worry,

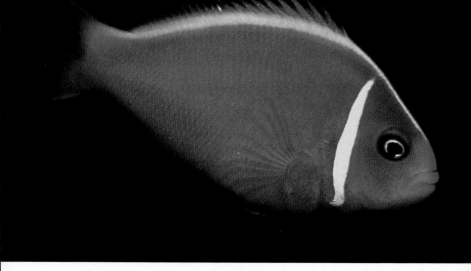

Skunk clowns are not particularly colorful but, due to their peaceful natures, often appeal to fish hobbyists.

though, these skunks won't stink up the aquarium. These hardy fishes are good for the beginner if they are introduced early because they tend to be a bit timid and easily overwhelmed by aggressive tankmates. The skunk clownfishes reach 3-3.5 inches in length.

Maldives Clownfish, *Amphiprion nigripes*
White-bonnet Clownfish, *Amphiprion leucokranos*
Thielle's Clownfish, *Amphiprion thiellei*

Although similar to the skunk clowns in body shape and color, the Maldives and White-bonnet Clownfish lack the characteristic stripe along the back. These two species are hard to find and difficult to keep in the aquarium. They are not recommended for the beginner. Thielle's Clownfish is a rare species that is not likely to be available to the home aquarist.

The white-bonnet clown (Amphiprion leucokranos) *is an uncommon species, so finding it in fish shops is a rare treat!*

The Clarkii Complex
Clark's Clownfish, *Amphiprion clarkii*

Reaching lengths in excess of 4 inches, Clark's Clownfish is a popular and hardy member of the clownfish clan. Adult color varies from yellow to dark brown with two or three white bands. This species is ideal for the beginner, but best suited to a larger aquarium because of its size.

Clark's clownfish (Amphiprion clarkii) *is actually a perfect species for beginners.*

**Barrier Reef Clownfish, *Amphiprion akindynos*
Allard's Clownfish, *Amphiprion allardi*
Two-band Clownfish, *Amphiprion bicinctus*
Chagos Clownfish, *Amphiprion chagosensis*
Orange-fin Clownfish, *Amphiprion chrysopterus*
Oman Clownfish, *Amphiprion omanensis*
Madagascar Clownfish, *Amphiprion latifasciatus***

There are seven other species of clownfish that are similar to Clark's Clownfish with two white bands on their bodies, but most are difficult, if not impossible, to attain. The Barrier Reef Clownfish, with its burnt orange color, is not only hard to find, but also not the hardiest of the clowns. The adult Allard's Clownfish is nearly black, but it is also not readily available for the average aquarist. Unfortunately, the same can be said for the Two-band Clownfish, with its beautiful dandelion-yellow coloration, and the Chagos Clownfish, which is only found on the remote Chagos Islands in the middle of the Indian Ocean. The widely distributed Orange-fin Clownfish has striking blue bands and reaches 5 inches, but it is not as hardy as the Clark's Clownfish. The Oman Clownfish has a unique forked tail,

The orange-fin clown (Amphiprion chrysopterus) *is a stunning clownfish and fairly easy to keep as well.*

but it is impossible to obtain. The Madagascar Clownfish, with its yellow, slightly forked tail, is not likely to be found in the aquarium trade.

Mauritian Clownfish, *Amphiprion chrysogaster*
Seychelles Clownfish, *Amphiprion fuscocaudatus*
Three-band Clownfish, *Amphiprion tricinctus*

These three species closely resemble the rest of the Clarkii Complex, but they always have three bands and dark tail fins. They are also very limited in their distribution, which inevitably makes them almost impossible to obtain. Both the Mauritian and the Seychelles Clowns have beautiful yellow bellies, while the colors of the Three-band vary from yellow to black.

The three-band clown (Amphiprion tricinctus) *can be found in large groups in nature.*

The Saddleback Complex

Saddleback Clownfish, *Amphiprion polymnus*
Wide-band Clownfish, *Amphiprion latezonatus*
Sebae Clownfish, *Amphiprion sebae*

These relatively rare aquarium species are not well suited for the beginner because they are very sensitive to stress, they are spooked easily, and they acclimate very slowly to aquarium living. The Saddleback Clownfish is dark colored with a saddle-like broad band at the mid-body and grows to about 4 inches. The Wide-band Clownfish ranges in color from brown to black with a very broad middle stripe. The Sebae Clownfish is also darker in color, but with two white bands and a yellow tail.

The saddleback clownfish (Amphiprion polymnus) *is relatively hard to find in the aquarium trade.*

This is the yellow-striped maroon clownfish (Premnas biaculeatus).

The Maroon Complex
Maroon Clownfish, *Premnas biaculeatus*

This is the only species of clownfish that does not belong to the genus *Amphiprion*. The Maroon Clownfish has two strains: yellow-striped and white-striped. Although a beautiful species, it is notoriously aggressive and has little tolerance for other Maroon Clownfish; it is not recommended for the beginner

Where do the Clownfishes Live?

The 28 species of clownfishes that I just described can only be found in the tropical Pacific and Indian Oceans. These waters include the South, Central, and Western parts of those oceans, as well as the Red Sea. There are no

Clownfishes live among soft corals like this Xenia *species.*

clownfishes in the Eastern Pacific and Atlantic Oceans, or the Mediterranean Sea. Some species, like the Madagascar Clownfish, occur in small, discrete areas, while others, like the Ocellaris Clownfish, are distributed over a broader geographic range.

Most saltwater fish in the aquarium trade are captured from their natural homes in the wild, transported across the world, and distributed to wholesale and local dealers in your neighborhood. This is not the case for most clownfishes, however, which are among the only species of saltwater fish routinely reared in captivity, or captive-produced. Therefore, the clownfish that you buy for your aquarium is not likely to have come from the Indo-Pacific, but probably from a professional clownfish breeder. This is good for the environment, good for the fish, and good for you.

The Life of a Clownfish

The life cycle of the clownfish is much more complicated than you would expect of this lovely little fish. You already know that clownfishes need anemones in order to survive in the wild, but I bet you didn't know that clownfishes could actually change sex from male to female!

The life of a clownfish starts with eggs, hundreds of them, that the female clownfish deposits on a hard surface near the anemone home. The bright-orange eggs are fertilized and tended by the male while the female guards the nest. After eight days of development, the eggs hatch and tiny 1/8-inch translucent larvae emerge and swim to the surface, attracted by the moonlight. For the next one or two weeks, the larvae will feed on tiny planktonic plants and animals, tripling in size and developing into tiny clownfishes. At this time, the micro-clownfishes settle to the bottom and seek a home in the tentacles of an anemone. Once the young clownfish has found an anemone, it's likely to spend the rest of its life on and about its new home. If a clownfish does not find an anemone, it will surely die in the mouth of a predator.

The life of the clownfish starts to become more complicated after it settles in an anemone. This is because clownfishes have social classes! The social hierarchy on the anemone typically includes one dominant mature female, a mature male, and a few juveniles on the lowest rungs of the ladder. If the new clownfish settles on an anemone that is already occupied, it assumes the lowest position in the hierarchy. The larger female and male fish dominate and intimidate the younger fish into submission, thereby keeping them small and immature. None of these smaller fish will reproduce until one of the dominant fish dies.

If, however, the new clownfish settles on an unoccupied anemone, it establishes its own household and grows rapidly into a mature male. When another clownfish of the same species arrives, the dominant male transforms into a female, the new fish matures into a male, and they mate for life. The cycle continues. If the dominant male dies, one of the immature fishes matures into a male. If the dominant female dies, the dominant male becomes a female. In all cases, the dominant female, which is usually larger, is the defender of the territory. The breeding couple will spawn about twice a month for years. In a healthy aquarium, clownfish will live for 10 to 20 years.

Clownfishes and Anemones

Any book on clownfishes has to include some basic information on their natural companions, the sea anemones. These "flowers of the sea", with their tubular bodies and soft tentacles, are actually animals closely related to corals and jellyfish. Like their relatives, anemones have no backbone, and so they are classified as invertebrates, as in "no-vertebrae". They also have specialized stinging cells called "nematocysts," which they use to capture prey like fishes and other invertebrates. The clownfishes have a remarkable relationship with the anemones: They are unaffected by the nematocysts. Therefore, they live, hide, and seek protection in the tentacles

Although there are about 1000 species of sea anemones in the world, only ten are natural hosts to clownfishes. In addition, each of the clownfish species will only live with specific anemone species. So, for example, the Percula Clownfish will associate with only three species of sea anemones. The ten sea anemones that host clownfishes belong to three families: Actiniidae, Stichodactylidae, and Thalassianthidae. Sea anemones, like many animals, have several common names that vary from place to place.

of an anemone for their entire lives. Scientists refer to this unique relationship as obligate symbiosis because the clownfish will die without the protection of the anemone.

The exact reason why clownfishes are immune to the anemone's stinging tentacles is not fully understood. Some feel that the fish secretes thick protective mucus, while others believe that the clownfishes smear themselves with the anemone's mucus. Another hypothesis contends that clownfishes are not stung because the anemone's tentacles cannot adhere to them. Whatever the reason, one thing is for certain: a clownfish without an anemone is a clownfish no more, unless it lives in an aquarium.

In the aquarium, clownfishes live quite well without a sea anemone host. In fact, I do not even recommend anemones for the beginner. Sea anemones are delicate invertebrates that are not hardy in the average marine aquarium. Many die after a few weeks or months and the aquarist is left frustrated, while the clownfishes continue to thrive. The bottom line is that anemones require high intensity lighting of the correct spectrum, strong current, trace elements in the water, correct nutrition from specialty foods, and excellent water quality.

For the adventurous hobbyist who insists on providing an anemone home for clownfish, I would take the following recommendations provided in Joyce Wilkerson's book,

The white stripe running down the dorsum of this orange skunk clown (Amphiprion sandaracinos)*is thought to be a form of camouflage while the fish is in an anemone.*

Clownfishes: A Guide to Their Captive Care, Breeding & Natural History. Choose one of the least fragile sea anemones, which include the Bulb Tentacle, Corkscrew Tentacle, and Haddon's Sea Anemones. Make sure that you choose a healthy specimen, which is not torn, sagging, bright white, unattached to the substrate, or refusing to feed. Don't expect to nurse an ailing anemone back to health, as it is simply not likely to recover. Be sure to provide adequate lighting, strong current, and proper anemone food. Your aquarium should be meticulously monitored for proper levels of calcium, specific gravity, alkalinity, trace elements, and temperature. If you intend to house anemones, I recommend that you refer to the books listed in the bibliography for more details on how to do so.

A number of other anemone-like invertebrates have been used by clownfishes in the home aquarium. These include mushroom anemones, leather and colt corals, elegance coral, and a few large-polyped stony corals like Frogspawn and Anchor Corals. Establish your aquarium before you complicate it with invertebrates.

The red and black clown (Amphiprion melanopus) *is a very beautiful and colorful species of clownfish.*

The Clownfishes and Their Anemones

Family Actiniidae

Anemone: Bulb Tentacle, Bubble Tip, Rose, Maroon Sea Anemone *(Entacmaea quadricolor)*

Clownfishes: Barrier Reef, Allard's, Two-band, Orange-fin, Clark's, Red Saddleback, Tomato, McCulloch's, Red and Black, Oman, Australian, Three-band, Maroon, Ocellaris

Anemone: Corkscrew Tentacle, Long Tentacle Sea Anemone *(Macrodactyla doreensis)*

Clownfishes: Mauritian, Clark's, Pink Skunk, Saddleback, and Maroon clownfishes.

Family Stichodactylidae

Anemone: Delicate, Sebae, Hawaiian, White Sand Sea Anemone *(Heteractis malu)*

Clownfishes: Clark's, Maroon

Anemone: Magnificent, Ritteri Sea Anemone
(Heteractis magnifica)
Clownfishes: Skunk, Barrier Reef, Two-band, Mauritian, Orange-fin, Clark's, White-bonnet, Red and Black, Maldives, Ocellaris, Percula

Anemone: Leathery, Sebae Sea Anemone
(Heteractis crispa)
Clownfishes: Barrier Reef, Two-band, Orange-fin, Clark's, Red Saddleback, Wideband, White-bonnet, Red and Black, Oman, Percula, Pink Skunk, Saddleback, Orange Skunk, Three-band

Anemone: Beaded, Aurora Sea Anemone
(Heteractis aurora)
Clownfishes: Barrier Reef, Allard's, Two-band, Mauritian, Orange-fin, Clark's, Three-band

Anemone: Haddon's, Saddle Carpet Sea Anemone
(Stichodactyla haddoni)
Clownfishes: Barrier Reef, Mauritian, Orange-fin, Clark's, Saddleback, Sebae, Allard's, Ocellaris, Percula

Anemone: Gigantic, Giant Carpet Sea Anemone
(Stichodactyla gigantea)
Clownfishes: Barrier Reef, Two-band, Clark's, Ocellaris, Percula, Pink Skunk, Australian

Anemone: Merten's, Merten's Carpet Sea Anemone
(Stichodactyla mertensii)
Clownfishes: Barrier Reef, Skunk, Allard's, Mauritian, Orange-fin, Clark's, Seychelles, Madagascar, White-bonnet, Ocellaris, Orange Skunk, Three-band

Family Thalassianthidae
Anemone: Adhesive, Sticky Carpet, Pizza Sea Anemone
(Cryptodendrum adhaesivum)
Clownfishes: Clark's, Tomato, Maroon

Chapter 2

Anatomy and Physiology of Clownfishes

General Anatomy

For the most part, the clownfishes have many of the same external characteristics shared by the majority of fishes. You know by looking at all 28 species of clownfishes that they are very similar looking and, therefore, you can see why they have been placed in the same family and, with one exception, genus. However, you can also see why they are considered different species—because of their colors and body shapes, among other reasons. Nonetheless, like all species of fishes, clownfishes have adapted to life in water, which is 800 times denser than air. To deal with this, fish have developed a variety of ways to move easier, breathe, and feed in a dense medium, which involves the body shape, fins, scales, and swim bladder.

The body shape of the clownfishes is clearly not built for speed. Instead, its oval body and large, rounded fins are typical of slower fishes that live in the safety of the coral reef, or, in this case, an anemone. The fins are important appendages that propel, stabilize, maneuver, and stop the fish. The supporting structures of fish fins are hard spines and soft rays; anyone who has handled a fish knows that the spines of the fins can be sharp. These bony structures offer some protection against predators. Some of the clownfish fins are paired like the pectoral and pelvic fins, which allow the fish to stabilize, turn, maneuver, hover, and even swim backwards. The unpaired, or median fins, are the dorsal and anal fins, which, in clownfishes, are the only fins with spines. Clownfishes have two kinds of dorsal fins, depending on the species. Some, like the Tomato Clownfish, have a single long dorsal fin, while others, like the Percula Clownfish, have two separate dorsal fins. The dorsal fin, like the anal fin, helps to stabilize the fish and keeps it moving straight. In most fishes, the caudal, or tailfin, propels the fish forward, but the broad, rounded caudal fin of the clownfish is certainly not ideal for prolonged bursts of speed. Instead, clownfishes use mostly their median and pectoral fins to move about; this is called labriform motion.

Scientists are still unsure of how clownfishes can tolerate the sting of sea anemones.

The body of the clownfish, like most fishes, is covered with scales. The scales are composed of a hard bony substance and serve to protect the fish, reducing the chance of injuries and infection. Covering the scales is a very thin layer of skin tissue that contains mucous cells. This mucous coating protects the fish against injury and infection, as well as helps the fish swim more easily in the water, reducing the friction between the body and the denser water itself. The scales of a fish are actually translucent, meaning they lack color. The vibrant colors of the clownfishes come from the specialized pigment cells called chromatophores, located deep in the dermal layer of the skin.

Maintaining a certain level in the water column without having to expend a lot of energy is very important to fish. Therefore, most species have special organs called swim bladders, also called gas bladders. This gas-filled sac located in the abdominal cavity of the fish acts as a life vest keeping the fish at the correct level in the water column.

Senses

Most species of fish have at least five senses, which they use to find food, avoid predators, communicate, and reproduce. The eyes of fishes are remarkably similar to our own, except they lack eyelids, their irises work much slower, and their eye lenses are spherical. With eyes located on the sides of their heads, clownfish have a wide field of view from head to tail, but cannot see much directly in front of them. Since fish eyes are adapted to slow changes in light intensity, sudden and rapid changes will startle and shock a fish. Therefore, gradual changes in aquarium lighting allow the fish to accommodate and avoid temporary blindness.

Sound carries much farther and faster in water than in air because water is a much more efficient conductor. Clownfishes, like most fish, don't possess external ears, but they do have inner ears. The auditory component of the inner ear consists of the saccule and the lagena, which house

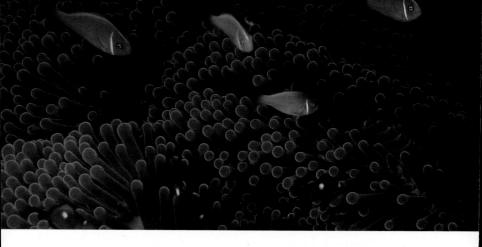

This group of pink skunk clowns (Amphiprion perideraion)
is living in a large sea anemone in waters off the Fiji Islands.

the sensory components of hearing, the otoliths. Sound vibrations pass through the water, through the fish's body, and reverberate off the otoliths in the inner ear, exciting sensory hair cells. These cells are also responsible for clownfish balance. Fish can also detect sound waves with a very specialized organ called the lateral line system, which detects disturbances in the water. Sensory receptors called neuromasts lie along the surface of the fish's body in low pits or grooves. The lateral line is visible along the sides of the clownfish, but you need to look very closely. This unique system helps the clownfish detect other fishes, sense water movement and currents, and avoid obstacles.

Clownfishes have the senses of smell (olfaction) and taste (gustation) to sense chemical cues in their environment. To smell, a clownfish has two sets of external nostrils, called nares, which draw water into the nasal sacs located above the mouth. In these olfactory pits, odors are perceived and communicated to the brain via a large nerve. The olfactory system of the fish is not attached to the respiratory system like in humans, but remains isolated from the mouth and gills. Smell is particularly important in prey and mate detection in clownfishes. Taste is generally a close-range sense in fishes and is especially helpful in the identification of food and noxious substances. The taste buds of fishes are not only found in the mouth, but also on the external surfaces of the skin, lips, and fins.

Feeding and Digestion

The mouth of the clownfish is terminal, meaning that the body terminates in a mouth that opens forward. This is typical of many reef fishes that snatch food from the water column. Since the size of the mouth is usually related to the size of the fish's preferred food, you can see that the small mouth of the clownfish is well designed for small invertebrates and algae. Most marine fish have a relatively straight-forward digestive system, which varies little from species to species. Food passes from the mouth, down the esophagus,

Skunk clowns vary greatly in their coloration intensity.

and into the stomach, where physical and chemical digestion occurs. Chemical digestion continues in the intestine where nutrients are absorbed.

Circulation and Respiration

Your clownfish, like all living creatures, needs oxygen to live. While we can simply inhale oxygen from the air that we breathe, fishes must extract oxygen from the water that surrounds them. This is the job of the gills, which have thin-walled membranous blood vessels that allow gas exchange between the blood and the water. On each side of a fish's head there are four gills that are protected by a singular gill flap or operculum. To breathe, and you will see this in your clownfish, a fish draws water into its mouth, then closes its mouth and forces the water over its gills and out the operculum. Fresh, oxygenated water flowing over the gills provides oxygen to the blood while removing wastes like carbon dioxide and ammonia. Since water contains much less oxygen than air, fish must breathe 10 to 30 times more water to get the same amount of oxygen. The respiration rate or breathing rate in clownfishes is about 65 to 75 breaths per minute. If the respiration rate of your clownfish is consistently higher, the oxygen level in your aquarium water is too low. Thus, checking the respiration rate in your clownfish is a good way to monitor its health.

The heart in the clownfish, like all fishes, circulates blood throughout the fish's body. Fresh arterial blood is pumped from the gills to the organs and tissues to keep them powered with oxygen. Venous blood that is loaded with carbon dioxide and ammonia is forced through the heart from these tissues to the gills where it is oxygenated.

Osmoregulation

Saltwater contains much higher concentrations of dissolved salt and other elements than freshwater. The concentration of these salts in water is referred to as its

This black percula clown (A. percula var.) *is a rare specimen that makes a great addition to any marine fish collection.*

salinity or specific gravity. A fish living in saltwater, like a clownfish, has less salts in its body than the surrounding water. This situation can create a real problem for the fish because osmosis causes water loss through the gills and skin. Therefore, marine fish are always threatened by the loss of water from their cells because their environment is more saline. To deal with this problem, clownfishes drink large quantities of water and eliminate salts in small amounts of highly concentrated urine and feces, as well as at the gills. This is called osmoregulation, which is important to understand for a few reasons: Clownfish burn a lot of energy to prevent the loss of water and excrete salt, so they require good nutrition and good health; the quality of water that your clownfish drinks must be excellent; and, abrupt changes in salinity will disturb the internal chemistry of your fish. Since clownfish are excellent osmoregulators, they can tolerate a specific gravity range of 1.017 to 1.030, but efforts should be taken to avoid abrupt changes.

Part Two

Keeping Clowns in Your Home

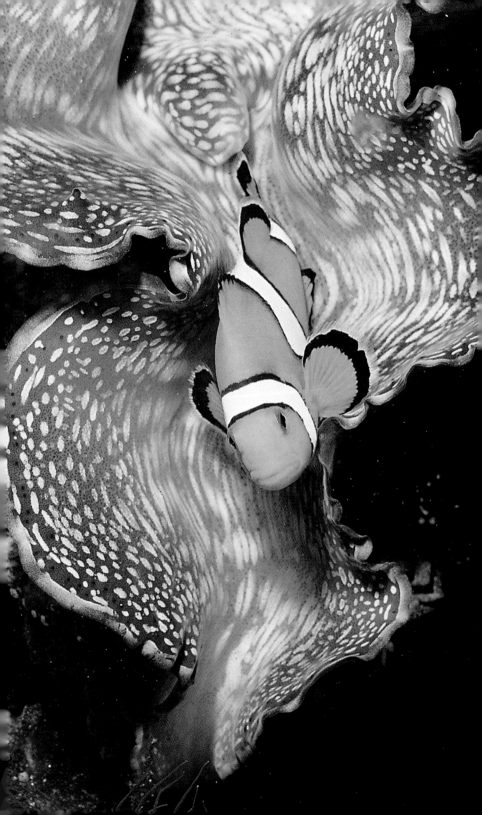

Chapter 3

The Clownfish Aquarium

Before you can keep clowns, you need to build a circus tent, so to speak. Whether you already have a freshwater aquarium or you are starting from scratch, this part of the book will provide you with enough information to establish a healthy marine environment for your clownfishes.

Tank Choices and Stands

Although all the components of the aquarium are essential, nothing is more important than the actual tank itself. Tanks come in many shapes, sizes, and styles, so take a little time to plan your aquarium before you buy. In doing so, consider where you intend to place it, how much money you want to spend, and the number and kind of clownfishes you want to keep. When you choose the right spot for your aquarium, make sure it is in a place where people will enjoy it and that it's not exposed to direct sunlight.

As far as tank size is concerned, the general rule of thumb is to buy the largest aquarium that you can afford and accommodate in your home. However, be mindful that a large aquarium is not essential for clownfishes because most remain close to their anemone homes (or surrogate anemone homes), therefore using very little tank space. Smaller species like the Ocellaris clownfish can be kept in tanks as small as 10 or 20 gallons, while larger clownfishes, like the Tomato Clownfish, are best suited for tanks of 40 gallons or larger. Also realize that the smaller the tank, the greater the chances of having water quality problems; larger tanks allow for mistakes in overfeeding. Larger tanks also accommodate more fish! To get an idea of how many fish your tank will hold, use the general rule of thumb of 1 inch for every 4 gallons of water for the first six months. This can be gradually increased to 1 inch for every 2 gallons. So, for example, a 40-gallon tank can hold 10 inches of fish or 10 one-inch Perculas, and, after six months, up to 20 inches of fish.

When it comes to tank shape, be sure to take into consideration the simple concept of surface area, which is the amount of area on the surface of the tank that is exposed to air. The more surface area, the more gas exchange, and,

The Clark's clown (Amphiprion clarkii) *is a great species to purchase as your first clownfish species.*

therefore, the more oxygen entering the water and toxic gases like carbon dioxide leaving the water, which will keep your clowns smiling. The shape of the tank dictates the amount of surface area. Tall, slender tanks do not have a lot of surface area relative to the volume of water, so you won't get a high rate of gas exchange. On the other hand, a short, wide tank will have more surface area and is better for gas exchange. They are also easier to clean and easier to work in.

Aquariums these days are either glass or acrylic. The choice is largely up to you. Glass aquariums are available in a variety of shapes and do not scratch as easily as acrylic aquariums do, but they are heavier. Acrylic aquariums are usually molded as a single piece, which makes them more transparent, but this will also distort your view at the corners. Acrylic is lighter than glass, offered in more shapes and sizes than standard glass aquariums, and tends to be stronger than glass. However, acrylic tanks do scratch easily and they can be quite a bit more expensive.

Don't forget to buy a hood or glass cover for your aquarium when you purchase the tank. This is an important piece of equipment because it keeps objects out of the tank, and it keeps fish, water, and heat in the tank. The hood, also called a canopy or cover, fits the dimensions of the tank and can be adjusted to allow for aquarium accessories. I recommend the type of hood that also houses the aquarium light. These units are properly designed to keep water from the lighting unit, which minimizes electrical hazard.

An aquarium full of water and loaded with filters, lights, gravel, and all the other accessories may be your heaviest piece of furniture in the house, so you need to support it properly. The aquarium stand is the best support for the massive weight of this system. Aquarium stands are generally manufactured out of wood, which can be very decorative, or wrought iron. If you decide to use a piece of household furniture, make sure that it can hold the weight; you don't want to see what happens if it collapses!

Although clowns are generally hardy, you must make sure your filters are always working their best to ensure premium water quality.

Types of Filters for Clownfish Aquariums

In the wild, clownfishes live in clear tropical waters where their wastes are readily swept away and naturally filtered. On the other hand, their products of digestion and respiration accumulate in your aquarium, which is a relatively small body of water compared to the ocean. These toxic substances will kill your clownfishes if you do not filter them from the tank. The aquarium filter either removes these substances from the water or converts them to less harmful compounds, which are returned to the aquarium. The basic filter contains filter media, which actually do all the work. These media need to be changed periodically to ensure that the filter is operating properly.

There are many kinds of filter systems that are suitable for clownfishes, which, for the most part, are pretty hardy little fish. But, if you are keeping your clowns with invertebrates like anemones or corals, then you will need to provide more complex filtration. When you choose a type of filter, make sure that it provides at least some level of mechanical, biological, and chemical filtration. Mechanical filtration physically removes suspended particles from the water by passing it through a fine filter medium. Biological filtration involves the bacterial conversion of toxic wastes into less harmful substances. Chemical filtration uses a chemical treatment like activated carbon to remove toxic substances from the aquarium. Fortunately, most commercially manufactured aquarium filters provide all three kinds of filtration, but with different levels of effectiveness.

The important thing to remember is that you must make sure that the size of your filter is well matched to the aquarium. For larger aquariums (over 20 gallons), it's a good idea to have more than one filter, and even a mixture of different kinds of filters, such as canister, undergravel, or trickle filters.

Undergravel Filters

The most common filter for the marine aquarium is the undergravel filter, which, after being around for so many years, is still an excellent choice of filtration. The basic undergravel filter consists of a perforated plastic plate that rests on the bottom of your aquarium tank under the gravel. Your aquarium gravel acts as the filter media, and water is circulated through it with lift tubes at each corner. Most undergravel filters are covered by two grades of gravel, fine grade on top of a coarse grade, separated by what is known as a gravel tidy. Once a healthy filtration system is established, this filter can be used for months as long as you clean the gravel on a monthly basis. Although most undergravel filters do not provide chemical filtration, carbon cartridges that fit on the lift tubes are now available. Undergravel filters are relatively inexpensive filters that provide excellent biological filtration for the clownfish aquarium. If you are going to use an undergravel system, reverse flow is the most efficient, either with powerheads or, preferably, with a canister filter.

Submersible Filters

The submersible power filter or sponge filter is great for the small clownfish aquarium. The filter is composed of sponge material, which provides surface area for mechanical and biological filtration. Submersible power filters can be driven by air, but those with powerhead pumps are much better. Sponge filters are inexpensive and easy to maintain because you simply rinse them in freshwater or saltwater. Although they come large enough to filter up to 125 gallons, I only recommend them for smaller tanks (up to 20 gallons).

External Filters

The external power filter is a plastic box that hangs on the outside of the tank and is powered by its own motor. The filter generally contains filter floss, filter sponges, biowheels, and activated carbon as filter media. These filter media provide mechanical and chemical filtration, while biological filtration is established as the filter matures and bacteria colonize it. The external power filter also circulates the water, providing valuable aeration. These are very simple filters to maintain, as most have cartridges that pop in and out. However, it's best to retain some of the used filter floss or use a sponge type media so that helpful bacteria can be kept. A single external power filter is fine for a small, 10 to 20 gallon tank, but may be used with an undergravel filter for larger tanks.

Canister Filters

The canister filter is an external power filter that sits on the floor or under the aquarium. It is a self-contained high-pressure pump that draws water from the aquarium and returns it to the tank or to another filter like the reverse flow undergravel filter. The filter contains compartments with various kinds of filter media, like activated carbon, filter sponges, filter floss, and ceramic bodies. Water is pumped over all the media layers and mechanical, chemical, and biological filtration is provided. These filters are more expensive yet provide excellent, efficient filtration at a very high rate. Moreover, they do not need to be cleaned as frequently.

Trickle Filters

The trickle filter, or wet-dry filter, is more popular for advanced saltwater aquarium systems. They provide excellent and efficient filtration and work well in the average clownfish aquarium. The trickle filter maximizes the exposure of the aquarium water to bacteria and air at the same time so that bacterial conversion of ammonia is extremely efficient. An overflow box on the back of your tank delivers water from the aquarium to the large acrylic box, which contains multiple layers of filter media for mechanical, biological, and chemical filtration. Another compartment contains a pump and other optional equipment, like heaters. Water from the aquarium is sprayed or trickled evenly over the first compartment through the filter media, where it collects at the bottom or sump, moves into the other compartment, and returns to the aquarium. Wet-dry filters provide maximum filtration as well as maximum aeration of the water.

Berlin System

Finally, the Berlin filtration system involves the use of live rock and live sand coupled with a protein skimmer. Live rock and live sand contain millions of bacteria that assist in the breakdown of ammonia and other harmful compounds. This is a natural form of biological filtration, which may be a bit too complex for the new clownfish aquarist. However, as your talents develop as an aquarist, your system may become more complex, and you may want to pursue this advanced method of filtration.

There are other kinds of water quality equipment available on the market, including the fluidized bed filter, in-line filters, diatom filters, denitrators, protein skimmers, UV sterilizers, and ozonizers. Many of these are considered overkill for the average clownfish aquarium unless your

clownfishes will be sharing space with invertebrates. The most common piece of equipment that is used in addition to the filter is a protein skimmer, which I recommend for larger clownfish aquaria. The protein skimmer will reduce tank maintenance, and your workload, by removing dissolved wastes like proteins and other organics.

Aeration

Filtration goes hand in hand with aeration, which is the process of adding oxygen to the aquarium water. You can have the cleanest water in the world, but your clownfishes will suffer if oxygen levels are low and carbon dioxide levels are high. You can aerate the water by simply increasing water circulation. In doing so, you are also evenly distributing the temperature of the water. Clownfishes prefer a moderate current, so increasing the circulation of water in your aquarium keeps them healthy.

While most filter systems aerate and circulate the water in some manner, it's a great idea to add additional aeration because you really can't have too much oxygen. An external air pump attached to airstones in the tank is an effective and attractive way to increase circulation. Keep a watchful eye on your airstones because they will degrade and clog over time. This will make your air pump work harder, increasing wear and tear. Airstones are relatively inexpensive, so replace them when the bubbles that they generate become inconsistent. Another important point that needs to be made regarding the use of airstones in marine aquariums is the density factor. Seawater is far denser than freshwater; therefore, airstones that are used in marine aquariums will put out a fine mist instead of the larger bubbles that you may be used to in freshwater aquariums. The fine mist,

Skunk clowns usually thrive in small groups.

coupled with heavy water flow, may give your aquarium a foggy appearance. If this is the case, consult your local aquarium dealer for an airflow control valve and adjust the amount of air that your air pump is feeding the airstone. Often, all that is needed is a little tweak of the lever and the problem is solved.

Lighting

Your clownfishes will need light, but only enough to keep them thinking that they live in a natural environment. In other words, your aquarium light will help your pets to set their biological clocks for feeding, resting, and, in some cases, breeding. Also, the light will help you to see your clownfish, which is not such a bad idea. Just like filtration, the type of lighting that you provide depends on what is

Excellent lighting will be needed should you decide to keep anemones with your clowns.

going to live in the aquarium. If you intend to keep a fish-only aquarium, with clownfishes and other fishes, then the most basic inexpensive aquarium light will work fine. However, if you intend to broaden the scope of your little ecosystem by adding invertebrates, then you should consider more advanced high-intensity lighting options.

Aquarium lighting fixtures come in a variety of styles, so make your choice when you plan your aquarium. The most basic aquarium light is the incandescent or tungsten light strip, which is not ideal for your clownfish aquarium because it produces heat, needs frequent bulb changes, and is more expensive to run. Instead, a fluorescent light strip is a better choice because it produces cool, even light, lasts months to years, and runs efficiently and economically. More advanced lighting options for reef tanks, which contain invertebrates, include power compact fluorescent, mercury vapor, and metal halide. To control your lighting to a natural day length of 12 hours, be sure to buy an inexpensive on/off timer switch. This will help you to simulate sunrise and sunset without having to remember to do it yourself.

Heating

Although your clownfishes may have originated in a breeder's tank, they are still tropical fish, and they need their home to be kept at tropical temperatures. Clownfishes can tolerate a temperature range of 64 to 90°F, but their natural home is about 80°F, which should be the temperature of their unnatural home as well. While maintaining an absolute temperature is important, it is more important to keep the temperature from fluctuating wildly or dramatically. Such inconsistency will shock or stress a fish and can potentially kill it.

Most of the heater choices on the market today will keep your aquarium temperature constant. There are two basic types: hanging heaters and submersible heaters. I prefer a submersible heater because you can put it near the bottom, out of the way of the aquarium's inhabitants, out of your view, and in a more efficient location for heat dispersion. You can even put the submersible heater in the sump of your trickle filter, keeping it completely out of the aquarium. In addition, most submersible heaters have advanced thermostat controls that make temperature selection and control easier. Regardless of the type, the correct-size heater for your aquarium can be found using the general rule of 5 watts per gallon of water up to 50 gallons. Since larger aquaria tend to hold heat better, 3 watts per gallon is enough power for tanks greater than 50 gallons. It is also a good idea to use two smaller heaters instead of one large one. This way, the tank will be heated more evenly, and, if one of the heaters fails, the other will prevent a dramatic drop in temperature. If you opt for more than one heater, simply divide the recommended power by two.

You should place your heater close to an area of high circulation so that heated water can be rapidly and evenly distributed throughout the tank. This is usually near the filter system, the filter input from an external filter, or the airstones. Also, be mindful that commercial heater settings should be tested before they are trusted. This is done by simply comparing the temperature setting to a thermometer reading and making adjustments as necessary. Therefore, make an aquarium thermometer an essential piece of equipment that you pick up with your heater.

Other Equipment

The basic aquarium setup for your clownfishes will include a number of other essential and non-essential items that you will want to buy in the beginning. Most of this equipment is standard to many fish-only saltwater aquariums and not specific to clownfish habitat requirements.

This is a very clean specimen of the pink skunk clown
(Amphiprion perideraion).

Substrate

One of the essential ingredients is aquarium gravel, which is typically a calcareous substrate like dolomite, calcite, aragonite, crushed coral, coral sand, or crushed shells. The gravel should be rinsed in freshwater before use, and a depth of about 1 to 2 inches is good for your clownfish aquarium.

Seawater

Of course, what good is an aquarium without water? You need to mimic natural seawater in the aquarium as closely as possible, and this is best done with a synthetic salt mixture, which is dissolved in ordinary tap water when you set up the aquarium.

Water Tests

To monitor and maintain the amount of salt in your saltwater, don't forget to buy a hydrometer, and while you're at it, pick up the basic water chemistry test kits like pH, ammonia, nitrite, and nitrate.

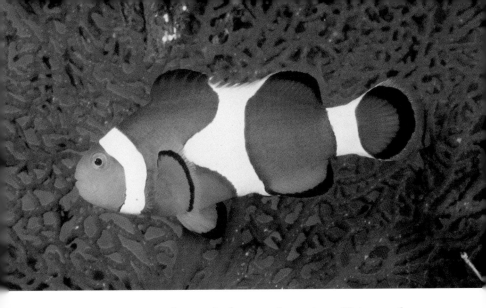

Sea fans make fantastic decorative additions to the marine fish aquarium.

Other Goodies

Of course, a bucket, net, gravel vacuum, siphon hose, and algae scrapper are all items that will come in handy when setting up and maintaining your aquarium. Most of the non-essential equipment has to do with how you want your aquarium to look when it is up and running.

Seascaping

You need to "aquascape" your aquarium by adding a background, tank decorations, and structure that will give your clownfish a natural sense of security. The typical fish-only aquarium has dead coral, tufa rock, lava rock, artificial coral, plastic seaweed, shells, or ornaments for decorations, but you can also add live rock and live corals if you have the right filtration and lighting.

Although deepwater reefs lack the visible variety of specimens that shallow water reefs contain, they are still strikingly beautiful.

Chapter 4

Setting Up the Aquarium

All of the pieces of your clownfish puzzle are ready, and now it's time to put them together. By now, you've spent a chunk of money and you have yet to see a single fish! Take your time and hang in there; you will want to make sure that everything is fine before you send in the clowns.

Aquarium Placement

Consider the placement of your aquarium to be a long-term decision, because once you set it up, it's not likely that you're going to move it. Therefore, choosing a permanent site for the aquarium is something you do not want to rush into. Make sure the right spot is in a place where people will enjoy it, that it's not in direct sunlight, and that it's close to power outlets.

Clownfish are playful fishes that respond to people in the room; they are basically show-offs. How much fun will it be for you or for them if you place their home in a room that is rarely used? At the same time, you don't want the aquarium in a room that is too active, like a child's playroom. Too much activity will spook your clowns, making them skittish and in a chronic state of stress. Too much sunlight will promote the growth of algae that can overwhelm your aquarium, so be careful not to place the tank too close to a window. And don't forget, without a readily available source of power, don't even bother to set up your aquarium.

STEP-BY-STEP Setup

Follow these ten simple steps and you will be well on your way to having a new clownfish aquarium.

1. Stands and Aquarium Placement

Set your aquarium stand in the chosen location, making sure that it is level, stable, and doesn't rock back and forth. Don't forget to leave enough room for air tubing, electrical cords, and any equipment that hangs on the back of the tank, like the filter, protein skimmer, and heater. After giving your new tank a quick freshwater rinse, place it on the stand so that it sits properly. This is also a good time to add an aquarium background if you decide to use one.

2. Filters

Set your filter in place but don't plug it in or fill it with water. If you have a submersible power filter, wait until your gravel is in place before putting it in the aquarium. Now is also a good time to set your protein skimmer in place.

3. Gravel and Ornamentation

After rinsing them in freshwater, add your gravel to the tank and set your rocks, coral, and other decorations in an attractive "aquascape".

4. Aeration and the Heater

Now is the time to add your airstones and run your air tubing from the aquarium to the airpump. Place the heater in an area of high circulation and make sure that you can see the indicator light. Do not plug in the air pump or the heater.

5. Water

To keep the water from trashing your well-decorated aquarium, place a large plate or bowl on the gravel. Fill your aquarium with tap water or pre-mixed saltwater, but make sure that the temperature of the water is about 80°F. Fill the tank to within an inch of the top and remove the bowl.

6. Water Conditioner and Salt

If your saltwater is not pre-mixed, add water conditioner and synthetic salt mix as per the instructions of the manufacturer. Test the specific gravity with the hydrometer, which should be about 1.023.

7. Hood and Lighting

Set the hood and lighting on top of the aquarium, adjusting other aquarium equipment as needed for it to sit properly.

Following the instructions closely with regard to your aquarium will help your clownfishes to thrive in their new home.

8. Power Up
Plug in and start your heater, filters, protein skimmer, air pump, and lighting.

9. Minor Adjustments
Over the next 24 hours, check your filters, temperature, and specific gravity, and adjust as needed. Your light cycle should be 12 hours per day and temperature should be at 80°F; specific gravity should range from 1.022 to 1.025.

10. Don't Add Fish
That's right, it's too early to add clownfish to your aquarium. You will need to let it mature, that is, let the water chemistry stabilize and allow for biological filtration to be established. Your new clownfish home needs to cycle.

The Nitrogen Cycle
By now, your aquarium is full of well-balanced clear tropical water that looks perfect for a clownfish, but it's just not ready. The problem lies in what you can't see, which are the bacterial colonies that will break down clownfish wastes. Clownfishes, like all fishes, are living creatures that require food for energy, burning it with the help of oxygen that they extract from the water with their gills. These biological processes produce toxic waste products, including ammonia and carbon dioxide, which are returned to the aquarium through the gills and in the urine and feces. You are also adding toxic waste to the aquarium when you overfeed because excess food is broken down into ammonia. These wastes need to be removed, and your biological filter will take care of it when it is up and running. The process of establishing your biological filter is called "cycling" your aquarium. In doing so, you are using what is referred to as the nitrogen cycle.

To accomplish the goal of removing ammonia from your aquarium, you will be harnessing the efforts of millions of

This mated pair of Clark's clowns (Amphiprion clarkii) *will need a well-balanced aquarium in order to continually mate and produce viable offspring.*

bacteria living in your biological filter. In reality, the ammonia is not removed, but it is converted to nitrite, which is in turn converted to nitrate, a less harmful compound. Specifically, the bacteria *Nitrosomonas* spp. convert ammonia (NH_4) into nitrite (NO_2), which is converted into nitrate (NO_3) by the bacteria *Nitrobacter* spp. A healthy aquarium depends greatly on the nitrogen cycle to reduce toxic ammonia into less toxic nitrogen compounds. But a new aquarium is very low on beneficial bacteria, so it has little to no biological filtration, and your new clownfish are likely to die from their own waste. Before you add more than a single fish, your aquarium needs to cycle through high levels of ammonia to high levels of nitrite to high levels of nitrate. Although nitrate is relatively harmless to fish, it must eventually be removed with frequent water changes.

The best way to monitor the cycling of your aquarium is to test for levels of ammonia, nitrite, and nitrate, as well as pH, which is a good indicator of a healthy aquarium. By following your test results, you will see these compounds cycle as your bacterial population builds and stabilizes. By the way, each time that you overload your aquarium with too much food or too many fish, it will cycle again and your fish will be at risk of suffering through the cycling process. If your aquarium is cycling when it is full of clownfishes, it is very important to reduce the amount of food dramatically to as little as one or two flakes per day per fish.

Final Steps to Clownfish

This next series of steps will take you from a new, beautiful, pristine aquarium to a well-cycled, new pristine aquarium with clownfishes.

1. About a week after you set up your aquarium, when all systems are running and temperature and specific gravity have stabilized, you can "seed" the aquarium. Seeding involves adding beneficial bacteria from an established aquarium into your new aquarium; this accelerates the nitrogen cycle. The bacteria may be added on filter media, like in a sponge filter, or by mixing gravel from an established aquarium to the surface of your gravel.

2. If your temperature reads 80°F, specific gravity reads 1.023-1.025, and pH reads 8.2-8.3, then you are ready to add a single clownfish to your aquarium. If your aquarium is 30 gallons or more, you may add a pair of clownfish. These clownfish should be fed sparingly once per day.

3. Test ammonia, nitrite, nitrate, and pH levels every two to three days. When your aquarium cycles, ammonia steadily increases, then declines as nitrite increases, which declines as nitrate increases. This period of cycling may take upwards of a month, so be patient.

4. When ammonia and nitrite levels have disappeared, you may slowly add more clownfishes or other tankmates to your aquarium. However, too many

Removing smaller volumes of water frequently will provide a well-balanced environment for your clowns.

fishes will cause your aquarium to cycle all over again, so be careful. In the first six months, do not exceed 1 inch of fish per 4 gallons of water. After six months, this may be increased to 1 inch of fish per 2 gallons, but not all at once.

5. Continue to test your water weekly for the next month, and then reduce testing to once every two weeks. Top up the water level of the aquarium with freshwater as needed. Replace about 25% of your aquarium water with pre-mixed saltwater every week for the first month, then monthly thereafter.

6. Follow the routine maintenance schedule, feed your fish, and, above all, enjoy your clownfish aquarium!

Chapter 5

Choosing Clownfishes

With an aquarium full of water and a whole bunch of equipment humming and buzzing away, there is something conspicuously missing—-a clownfish! There are 28 species of clownfishes, but which one is right for you?

Suitable Clownfish Species

There are a few things to consider when you decide which clownfishes will grace your aquarium. First and foremost, which ones tickle your fancy? While many of the clownfish species look alike, there are clear differences between the clownfish complexes. The Percula Clownfish may be the most popular, but it may not be your favorite. Of course, the availability of a species will clearly dictate whether or not you can even attempt to bring one home. We know from Chapter 1 that not all of the 28 species of clownfishes are available to the average aquarist. Furthermore, I don't recommend that you go out of your way financially to obtain a hard-to-get species until you have honed your aquarium-keeping skills. Chapter 1 also showed us that certain clownfish species simply do not fare well in captivity. Some species are not hardy, while others don't get

These juvenile clowns are very small and will need some more grow-out time before they are ready to be sold.

along with each other or their tankmates. Take this into consideration. Finally, the size of your aquarium will dictate the kinds of clownfishes as well. The larger species, like the Tomato Clownfish, require the aquarium space of at least 40 gallons. So, if your aquarium is only 10 gallons, you have to stick with the smaller species, like the Percula.

To give you an idea of which species are best for beginners and which ones are to be avoided altogether, I've divided the 28 clownfish species into two general groups according to whether or not they are recommended for beginners. To find more specific details about each species, refer to Chapter 1. The clownfishes recommended for beginners include: Ocellaris, Percula, Red and Black, Tomato, Red Saddleback, Skunk, Pink Skunk, Orange Skunk, and Clark's. The clownfishes that are rare, difficult to obtain, or not easy to keep include: Australian, McCulloch's, Maldives, White-bonnet, Thielle's, Barrier Reef, Allard's, Two-band, Chagos, Orange-fin, Oman, Madagascar, Mauritian, Seychelles, Three-band, Saddleback, Wide-band, Sebae, and Maroon.

Compatible Clowns

According to Joyce Wilkerson, whose book, *Clownfishes*, is one of the finest, the best companion for a clownfish is another of the same species. Therefore, if you intend to keep more than one clownfish, and you should, then keep two or more of the same kind. These fishes are very social and we know that they establish a hierarchy. This is very likely to happen in your aquarium among juveniles until a dominant female emerges. During this time, there will be much harmless fanfare as they try to intimidate and challenge each other. Once a hierarchy is established, the clownfish become a tight group, rarely leaving each other. However, if two dominant mature females are placed together, they are likely to stake out separate territories to avoid each other. Of course, if one or more of your clowns remains overly intimidated and shows signs of stress, it should be removed from the aquarium.

The Maroon Clownfish has little to no tolerance for others of the same kind. Efforts should be taken to avoid having more than one in an aquarium, unless you are trying to breed them.

Wild or Captive-raised?

Although most of the tropical marine fishes in the aquarium trade are taken from the wild, the clownfishes are among a handful of species that are reared in captivity. As I noted earlier, this is great because they are not exposed to the same kinds of stress. For example, a clownfish that is captured in the wild is collected on the other side of the world, double-bagged, and boxed for shipment, which can take days. These clownfish are not only heavily stressed, but they may be older, not accustomed to people, and not acclimated to life in captivity. On the other hand, tank-reared clownfish are used to life in an aquarium, they're used to having people take care of them, and they're much

Some clowns that are produced in captivity, such as this skunk clown, display unusual color variation.

younger, usually less than a year old. Moreover, they don't have to travel far to get to your dealer, so they are not as heavily stressed. Remember, stress can kill a clownfish! Finally, the less fish we catch from the wild, the more fish are left in the wild, and that's a good thing.

All of the clownfish species that I recommend for beginners have been successfully raised in captivity. You shouldn't have a problem finding tank-reared clownfishes at your local dealer, and certainly don't be afraid to ask.

Selecting and Buying a Healthy Clownfish

The first step to choosing the right clownfish is choosing the right dealer! With the growth of large superstores in today's society, there are more and more opportunities to buy fishes. This is great as long as you are able to establish a good working rapport with the store personnel. Take the time in the beginning of your new venture to meet a dealer who will take good care of you and who takes care of his fishes. In general, look for a dealer who carries and specializes in saltwater fishes, who maintains a good clean business, has healthy fish in his aquariums, and is always willing to answer your questions and spend time with you. A good dealer will give you invaluable information on reliable products and is motivated to help you maintain your system correctly.

Once you have a responsible and trustworthy dealer, the key to choosing a good clownfish is selecting a healthy clownfish. Select fish from healthy looking aquariums with clear water, clean panes, and no dead fish in the tank. Inspect the fish for signs of fatigue, disease, and stress. A healthy fish has clear eyes and skin, good balance in the water column, and clean, healthy fins that respond rapidly as the fish moves. Look for possible symptoms of disease, such as white granular spots, cottony white patches, frayed fins, or dull skin. The stomach of the clownfish should be rounded, not pinched. Healthy fish swim horizontally in a lively manner

Always look for a plump body and clean, unclamped fins when purchasing a clownfish (or any other fish, for that matter).

and are not shy. You can also evaluate the health of the animal by watching it feed. If a fish feeds in captivity, it's a pretty good sign that it's well adapted to its surroundings and its aquarium is clean and healthy. Finally, make sure that the fish has not just arrived, as it may still be suffering from travel stress.

Taking Your Clownfish Home

Once you have chosen your clownfish, your dealer will net the fish and place them in a bag containing water from the aquarium. A properly bagged fish will have water in about two thirds of the bag and air in the remaining space. On the trip home, make every effort to keep the bag from jostling too much and don't expose it to dramatic changes in temperature, like the car heater or direct sunlight. If you have a very long trip home, it's a good idea to pack the clownfish bag into a cooler, but don't add ice. The insulated cooler will keep the bag from losing and gaining heat.

Clownfishes will often need several days to acclimate to their new surroundings after you bring them home.

As soon as you get home, take care of your new clownfish immediately. Many seasoned aquarists have a quarantine tank for new fish to reside in until they are deemed healthy. This keeps the new clownfish, if not well, from causing problems for the main aquarium. Most beginners, however, don't have large, sophisticated aquariums that can be disrupted easily, so they introduce the new fish without quarantine.

The steps to getting the clownfish from the bag to the aquarium are pretty simple. First, float the unopened bag in your aquarium for 10 to 15 minutes so that its temperature acclimates to that in the aquarium. Then, open the bag, let air in and add about a cupful of water from your aquarium to the bag and let it sit for another 10 to 15 minutes. Then, add the fish to the aquarium by simply and gently scooping out the fish with a soft net, being careful not to add too much of the dealer's water, and place him in the tank right away. This procedure allows the fish to acclimate slowly to the chemistry and temperature of your aquarium's water.

Don't forget that you should not introduce too many fish at once, just one or two in the beginning and then a couple at a time after the aquarium cycles. This not only keeps your aquarium from cycling again, but it allows your clownfishes to get to know their surroundings and their new tankmates. There may be some aggressive behavior between new arrivals and clownfish that have set up territories, but this is to be expected.

Part Three

Caring for Your Clownfish

Chapter 6

Food and Feeding

Well, you have a beautiful little clownfish in your aquarium, but you need to keep it happy and healthy so that you can enjoy it for years to come. The first step, of course, is to feed it, and the key to feeding a clownfish is not to overfeed. If one thing can be said about the eating habits of clownfishes, it's the fact that they would feed all the time if given the opportunity. You couple that with their natural tendency to be little actors and actresses and you have a bunch of full-fledged beggars on your hands. It's up to you to muster the power to say no and to stick with a feeding regimen.

Types of Foods

Like all living things, your clownfish need proper nutrition and a well-balanced diet. This must include the basic raw materials for sustenance, growth, and reproduction. Clownfishes are omnivorous, which means that they will eat a variety of foods, including both meat and vegetables. The important thing is that they get the necessary nutrients from proteins, carbohydrates, lipids, vitamins, and minerals. Unfortunately, the exact dietary requirements of clownfishes are not fully understood, so it is essential to feed them a variety of foods so that the fish are most likely to obtain all their nutritional requirements.

Proteins are major constituents of all animal tissue, and they are essential to maintain normal growth. Carbohydrates are broken down into units of glucose, which is a major source of energy, and they can also be converted to lipids for energy storage. Lipids, or fats, are critical components of cell membranes and provide an immediate supply of chemical and stored energy. Vitamins and minerals provide the necessary ingredients for proper metabolism and skeletal stability. Carotenoids are pigments that give your clownfish their beautiful coloration; these should be included in their diets as well.

You can provide the right diet for your clownfish from several types of food, including commercially prepared foods, natural foods, and live foods. Remember, the key to proper nutrition is variety, so it's best to feed your clownfish a little bit of each throughout the week.

All clownfishes are opportunistic feeders, meaning that they will feed on whatever edibles happen to be close by.

Prepared Foods

Prepared foods come in a variety of forms, including flakes, tablets, and frozen mixtures. They are simple and easy to feed to your clownfishes, so there is a real temptation to use them exclusively. Although they do contain many of the essential nutrients, this is not the best feeding strategy, and your clownfish will not be getting everything they need. These foods are good as a staple, but you should make every effort to substitute other foods to enrich your fish.

Natural Foods

Natural foods are not heavily processed and may be fresh, frozen, or freeze-dried. These include fresh fish and invertebrate meat, as well as frozen or freeze-dried invertebrates. Frozen shrimp, squid, scallops, krill, plankton, brine shrimp, and glassworms are just a few of the natural foods available for your clowns. Freeze-dried brine shrimp is an excellent alternative to live culture. You can also feed your clownfish bits of common table seafood like shrimp and squid, but cooking or freezing them is a good idea because raw seafood can carry infectious diseases that might be transmitted to the clownfish.

Live Foods

Live foods are one of the best sources of nutrition for your clownfish. Clownfish that are fed live foods ordinarily grow faster and have vibrant colors and higher survival rates. Some live foods, like rotifers, may be obtained from your dealer, but others, like mosquito larvae and brine shrimp, can be cultured at home. You can collect mosquito larvae in the spring, summer, and fall by placing a tub of freshwater outside where the mosquitoes will lay their eggs. Simply collect the tiny larvae with a very fine mesh net and feed them to your clownfish.

The Brine shrimp (*Artemia* spp.) are tiny, shrimp-like invertebrate that are an excellent source of lipids and

Maroon clowns will often accept sporadic offerings of livebearer fry or live blackworms to round out their diets.

proteins. Of all the live food available, they are the safest because they do not carry disease. You can culture brine shrimp at home using the following steps.

1. Make up a hatch solution by filling a container with saltwater from your last aquarium change or mixing some to a specific gravity of 1.010-1.020 and a temperature of 75-80°F; add an aerator.

2. Add the brine shrimp eggs, called cysts, at a concentration of about 1 teaspoon of eggs per gallon of hatch solution; after 10 minutes, illuminate the container with a 40 watt light about 8 inches from the container for about 10 minutes. This will initiate hatching.

3. After 24 hours, shut off the aerator and allow the empty shells and unhatched eggs to separate from the hatchlings, which are called nauplii.

4. After 15 minutes, the nauplii can be attracted to a corner of the container using a small flashlight.

5. When they are concentrated, drain or siphon them into a fine mesh net.

At this point, the brine shrimp can be fed to your fish or placed in a container of saltwater for rearing to larger sizes. If you choose to keep the young shrimp, bring the water temperature to about 86°F, provide low aeration, and sunlight. The nauplii can be fed brewer's yeast, powdered rice bran dissolved in water, or algae that bloom in the container. It takes about two to three weeks to raise a colony of adult brine shrimp.

The Right Time to Feed

In the wild, clownfishes feed whenever they can, darting in and out of their anemone home to snag a tidbit of food, such as a small shrimp. Each time the clownfish does this, it risks being consumed by a larger predator. Life may be a bit different in the safety of your aquarium, but the voracious clownfish will still eat whenever it gets a chance. The general rule is to feed your clownfish and other tank inhabitants twice a day, once in the morning and once in the evening.

This false percula clown (Amphiprion ocellaris) *has just fed his host anemone a small piece of food.*

This generally coincides with your work schedule as well. Once you establish this feeding regimen, your clownfish will readily adapt to it, so try not to alter it too much. When you enter the room to feed your fish, they will dance and wiggle in anticipation. Just because you might have a day off, don't feed your fish at other times. If the kids are feeding the fish, stress to them the importance of maintaining the right schedule.

The Right Amount to Feed

In general, slowly offer as much food as your clownfish will eat in five minutes, and feed your fish in very small portions. Keep in mind that it is much better to feed too little than to feed too much. In reality, a clownfish can live for over a week without eating, so one day without food is fine. Any food that is not consumed will ultimately end up as ammonia, which will degrade your water quality. If you are feeding your clownfish flakes, one or two flakes per fish is enough. If flakes are sinking all the way to the bottom, you are feeding too much! If any food is left over after the five-minute period—you are an over-feeder.

Pay attention to your fish during feeding because this is a time to learn a lot about their health. Try to get a feel for who is eating and who is not. Refusal to eat is one of the first signs of illness, so keep an eye out for fish that seem to have no interest in food.

Remember to offer a variety of foods over the course of a week. Flake food and frozen brine shrimp may be your staples, but mix in different foods a couple of times a week.

Feeding During Aquarium Cycling

You will recall from Chapter 4 that your aquarium is extremely sensitive to ammonia when it is cycling. The addition of food to the tank will dramatically affect the cycle. Therefore, you need to minimize the amount of food for your clownfish while the aquarium is cycling. This is the

This rare species of clownfish is the wide-banded clownfish (Amphiprion latezonatus).

only time not to offer a variety of foods. Instead, restrict your fish's diet to one or two flakes of food per day.

Feeding While Away

If you are going to be away for one or two days, your clownfish will be fine without food. When you return, don't overfeed them because they missed a meal or two.

If you plan to travel for longer periods, either arrange to have somebody feed your fish or purchase an automatic feeder, which dispenses dry food. If a friend is going to take care of your pets, keep it simple and prepare portions ahead of time.

Chapter 7

Maintaining Water Quality

With an aquarium full of clownfish that are happy and healthy, it's very important to keep them that way. In this chapter (and the next) you will learn about the basic maintenance of fish-keeping. None of this is complicated, and with a few simple steps, you can keep your fish alive and swimming for years to come.

During the aquarium setup, we touched on a number of important concepts relative to the nitrogen cycle, salinity or specific gravity, and temperature. Just because your aquarium has cycled, your temperature is stable, and your specific gravity is constant, it doesn't mean that these parameters don't need to be continuously monitored. This monitoring requires test kits. They are relatively inexpensive and simple to use. Taking the time to test your water will ultimately tip you off to potential problems and save you the hardship of possibly losing your fish.

Nitrogen

In an established aquarium, a flourishing colony of beneficial bacteria is able to handle the ammonia load produced by your clownfish. If this load is dramatically increasing

Your testing will tell you when the aquarium is cycling again because your ammonia levels will rise dramatically. If this happens, reduce your feeding levels and conduct a 25% water change.

because of too many fish or overfeeding, the bacteria will be overburdened and the aquarium will cycle. You need to know this because an aquarium that is cycling needs to be treated with some care. Therefore, it's important to routinely monitor an established aquarium for ammonia, nitrite, and nitrate levels. If your aquarium simply houses clownfish, then a monthly test should be sufficient. However, if you have more sensitive tankmates, like invertebrates, or if you sense a problem with your fish, test your water more frequently.

Specific Gravity

The chemical composition of seawater is extremely consistent throughout the world. Although seawater is made up of 96% pure water (one atom of oxygen bonded with two atoms of hydrogen: H_2O), it also contains many dissolved minerals and salts. Of the remaining 4% of seawater's makeup, sodium and chlorine constitute 85% of the balance. Magnesium, sulfate, calcium, and potassium make up another 13%, while bicarbonate and 68 other elements make up the remaining 2% in very small quantities.

In your aquarium, you are mimicking seawater as closely as possible and you need to make sure that the amount of salt in your water is correct. There are a couple of ways to measure the amount of salt in saltwater.

Salinity refers to the actual concentration of salt in the water; it's not influenced by temperature, and it's expressed

Clownfishes are tolerant of wide ranges of specific gravity.

as a ratio of parts-per-thousand (ppt). Although the specific gravity of a liquid is directly related to temperature and your hydrometer may not be calibrated to the temperature in your aquarium, precise measurements are not as important as consistency. The easier and more practical way to measure the level of salt in your tank is to estimate specific gravity with a testing tool called a hydrometer, which is what you should have already purchased specifically for this purpose.

Specific gravity is actually the ratio of the density of the aquarium water to that of pure water at various temperatures. However, since the specific gravity of a liquid is directly related to temperature, your hydrometer may not be calibrated to the temperature in your aquarium. Specific gravity should be established in the range of 1.021 and 1.024, but more importantly, it should not be allowed to fluctuate dramatically because large changes can cause problems for your clownfish.

Monitor your specific gravity every couple of days. By far, the greatest change in salt level is caused by water evaporation from the tank. When the water evaporates in a saltwater aquarium, the salt remains in solution and becomes more concentrated, and the salinity and specific gravity increase. Watch your aquarium water level and refill it with freshwater weekly (or as needed) to keep your specific gravity as stable as possible.

Acid and pH

In Chapter 4, I mentioned the importance of measuring and monitoring your aquarium pH, which is actually the amount of acid in your aquarium. However, in contrast to what you may think, the lower the pH, the more acid is in your aquarium water. Saltwater is less acidic than freshwater, and your aquarium pH should be maintained between 8.1 and 8.3, compared to most freshwater aquaria that are commonly maintained between 6.5 and 7.5. (Exceptions include aquaria housing African cichlids and others that require hard,

You should routinely test the pH of your water when you test for nitrogen compounds. Any sudden drop in pH may require an increase in aeration and a partial water change. Regular water changes should maintain your pH at correct levels by removing nitrogenous compounds and replenishing your aquarium water.

alkaline water.) A drop in pH translates to an increase in the acidity of your aquarium water, and this is very harmful to your fish. The pH will drop in your aquarium if the amount of carbon dioxide and fish wastes increase. The accumulation of either or both of these will cause the water to acidify and the pH to drop. In fact, the nitrogen cycle itself will often produce acids that will alter the pH of your aquarium by causing it to either fluctuate or decrease over the course of the cycling period.

Because water chemistry is so important, potential clownfish owners should take time to learn the basics.

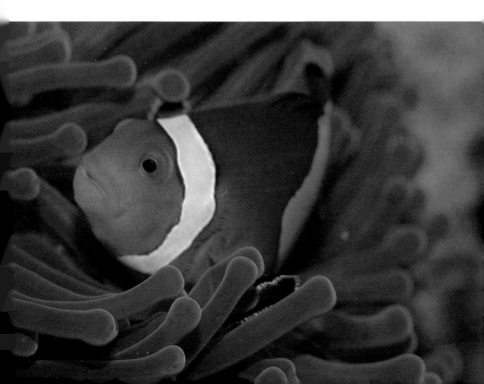

Other Chemical Factors

There are a variety of other water tests available, and these can be a bit confusing for the beginner. The extent to which you test these parameters depends on the complexity of your aquarium. If you stick with a simple clownfish aquarium, then nitrogen and pH testing should be sufficient to maintain the health of your pets. However, if you expand your aquarium to include invertebrates like anemones and corals, then you need to not only increase the quality of your filtration, but also monitor other water chemistry.

These other parameters include carbonate hardness, calcium, phosphate, and copper. Carbonate hardness refers to the buffering capacity of your aquarium water, and this is indicative of potential problems with pH. Calcium levels are important for invertebrates because many extract calcium from the water to build their calcium carbonate skeletons and shells. Phosphate is a natural fertilizer for algae, which can smother a reef system if out of control. Finally, copper is a common treatment for disease and toxic to invertebrates, so it is important to know how much is in the tank.

Algae

Inevitably, your aquarium will cultivate algae, which can be both good and bad.

In moderation, algae can be very beneficial because they assimilate nitrates and excess nutrients from the water, and your clownfishes may even snack on it from time to time.

Algae are actually not plants; they just act like them because they are photosynthetic organisms that occur throughout the world in many freshwater and marine habitats. They range in size from single-celled organisms to large seaweeds (kelp) that grow to over 230 feet tall. Generally, they are very hardy organisms with a tremendous capacity to reproduce. Algae can enter your aquarium as algal spores borne by the air, or carried by tank furnishings or water from another aquarium. In the ocean ecosystem, algae are important primary producers at the base of the food chain. You may notice that algae do not have roots and shoots like plants, but they may have root-like attachment structures and leaf-like fronds.

In your aquarium, algae inhabit the water's surface, are suspended in the water column, or grow on the surfaces of the aquarium's glass, rocks, gravel, coral, and tank decorations. Like plants, algae need light and nutrients to be successful. In your aquarium, strong lighting and nitrate from the nitrogen cycle fuel the propagation of algae, allowing them to act as convenient organisms that can be used to remove excess nutrients from your aquarium. Therefore, routinely scraping some of your algae from the tank will physically remove nitrates, phosphates, and other nutrients. .

Many new aquarists think that a sterile-looking aquarium is a clean and healthy aquarium, so they remove as much of the algae as they can at all times to keep it looking pristine. This is simply not true because algae are an integral part of the natural coral reef ecosystem. So, get accustomed to seeing algae and promoting algal growth in your aquarium. In a well-balanced aquarium, algae will remain in check and you will need to routinely remove some to maintain a clear view of your pets and to get rid of excess nutrients that it can add to your aquarium's bioload.

If your aquarium algae run amuck and get out of control, they will literally choke an aquarium by consuming oxygen during the night. When algae become a nuisance, consider this a sign that something is wrong in your aquarium. First, make sure your aquarium is not getting too much light. Sunlight from a nearby window, excessive aquarium lighting, incorrect aquarium lighting, and an aging light bulb will contribute to the problem. However, excess algal growth is usually caused by a problem with nutrient levels, so check your water chemistry for high nitrates. You may need to conduct a water change, increase aeration, or change your filter media.

Chapter 8

Routine Maintenance

In the wild, Mother Nature takes great care of the clownfishes. All of their wastes are swept away, their water is clean, and they can tend to the business of feeding, not getting eaten, and making more little clownfishes. In your home, you have to act like Mother Nature for your clownfishes. With the help of a filter, aeration, a protein skimmer, and all the other equipment that you may have working on your clownfish's aquarium, the job of keeping their water clean is much easier. But to keep this equipment working efficiently, you have to lend a helping hand. This is called simple preventative maintenance.

There are a few simple tasks that you should tend to on a regular basis. How often you clean your aquarium depends on how dirty it gets, and that depends on the number of fish, the efficiency of your filtration, and the amount of overfeeding.

Water Changes
Even in a well-balanced, perfectly tuned aquarium with an efficient biological filter, you will need to conduct water changes. This is because nitrate and other metabolites will slowly accumulate. Algae and certain bacteria will definitely

consume some of the nitrate, but not all of it. Thus, it must be physically removed before toxic concentrations are reached. Water changes also act to replace the resiliency of your aquarium water because certain chemical constituents and trace elements, like buffering capacity, are depleted over time and need to be restored.

The typical water change is about 10-20% of the tank's volume every month. The water that you add should be properly balanced, premixed saltwater with the same specific gravity and temperature, so as not to shock your fish. The amount you change depends on the quality of your filtration, the amount that you feed, and the number of fishes and other critters. If your aquarium has a lot of occupants or you tend to overfeed, a 20% change is in order. However, if your aquarium is not heavily stocked and you are very careful when you feed, 10% should be sufficient. You can also make smaller water changes more frequently, like 5% every one to two weeks.

By far, the most efficient way to conduct a water change is to use an aquarium vacuum and a large plastic bucket. The vacuum will allow you to clean your gravel while you draw water from the aquarium, with gentle stirring of the gravel. When you change the water, make every effort to efficiently clean as much of the gravel as possible, but don't rush over spots; there is always next time.

Vacuuming Your Tank

Getting the waste out of your gravel is one of the most important tasks of preventative maintenance. By doing so, you keep your biological filters from becoming overwhelmed and, hence, you can avoid tank cycling. If wastes are allowed to accumulate to excessive levels, your filter will clog and water quality will degrade rapidly.

Gravel vacuums, also called substrate cleaners, are available at your aquarium dealer. As I mentioned above, it's not a bad idea to vacuum your gravel when you conduct a routine water change, thereby accomplishing two tasks at once. Gently rake the gravel when you vacuum, being careful not to disrupt the filter media of an undergravel filter.

Filter Maintenance

With so many filter types available, it's difficult to describe the maintenance of a generic filter. Regardless, most filters last months with little care other than some simple cleaning. How much you clean your filter depends on the kind of filtration that it provides. A filter that is strictly mechanical can be cleaned thoroughly to remove debris, but a biological filter should not be touched very often. Filters that provide chemical filtration should be recharged every month.

If you have an undergravel filter and it is well established, it can be used indefinitely with some simple maintenance. Fortunately, with no filter floss or carbon to change, you only need to vacuum the gravel when you conduct a water change. Other care for the undergravel filter includes making sure that the airstones or powerheads are not clogged. Submersible power filters or sponge filters can be cleaned every two weeks to a month by simply rinsing them in freshwater, but don't wash them too thoroughly because you want to keep the bacteria. Most external power filters have cartridges that can be replaced monthly, but you should retain some of the media so helpful bacteria are not lost; activated carbon should be replaced every month as well. Canister filters should be cleaned monthly or bi-monthly. .

Like the undergravel filter, trickle (wet-dry) filters require very little maintenance. Every month, carbon should be replaced and sponges and filter pads should be rinsed, while bio-balls and ceramic bodies can be rinsed every six months to a year. The protein skimmer requires some daily care to make sure that it is working properly and to empty the collection cup if needed.

The Maintenance Schedule

The following is a checklist of your daily and weekly maintenance duties. Use this as a starting point and fine-tune it to fit your own schedule. Most of these simple steps require just a few minutes of your time, but will ultimately save you time in the long run.

Daily

1. Turn the aquarium lights on and off or use an automatic timer.
2. Feed your clownfish twice a day and remove any uneaten food.
3. Check your clownfish for signs of stress, disease, or death.
4. Check the water temperature and specific gravity and adjust as needed.
5. Empty the protein skimmer collection cup if necessary.
6. Check water level and top off as needed.
7. Make sure all aquarium systems are running smoothly (heater, filters, air pump).

Every Two Weeks

1. Remove excess algae as needed.
2. In an overstocked aquarium, clean filters and conduct partial water change.
3. Vacuum the aquarium gravel.

Monthly

1. Clean filter and replace filter carbon.
2. Test water chemistry.
3. In an average aquarium, conduct partial water change with gravel vacuum.

Long-Term

Unlike the freshwater aquarium, the marine aquarium

does not need to be completely broken down because a well-established biological filter will last for years. However, the undergravel filter may become heavily clogged over a long period and the gravel itself may begin to break down in about two years. Therefore, slowly replace the gravel over several months by removing a thin strip of gravel and replace it with new gravel. The following week, repeat the procedure and so on until the entire substrate has been replaced without disrupting the aquarium. Only break down your aquarium if you have an extreme emergency.

Emergencies

By definition, nobody can really plan for an emergency, but it's nice to know what to do if one occurs. The most common emergencies are power failure, aquarium leaks, overheating, and pollution.

Power Outages

Power outages can occur frequently in some areas, but most are temporary, lasting less than 12 hours. Your clownfish will be fine during short power outages. However, longer periods in excess of 12 hours will require some attention. In these cases, a battery-powered air pump will aerate the water to maintain dissolved oxygen levels. To prevent the loss of heat, a thick blanket or sleeping bag should be wrapped around the tank. Do not feed your fish while the power is down because the filters are down as well. If you live in an area prone to frequent power failures, you may consider the purchase of a portable generator for your aquarium.

Aquarium Leaks

If your aquarium springs a leak due to seam failure or impact from an object, collect as much water as possible into buckets and place your clownfish into them. Aerate the water, then rush out and replace the tank as soon as possible.

After you transfer the filtration and all other equipment, including your gravel, add the water and clownfish.

Overheating

A malfunction of your heater can cause your aquarium to overheat. Clownfishes can tolerate water temperatures as high as 90°F, but the radical change in temperature may kill them. You can avoid overheating by using two smaller, less powerful heaters instead of one large one. Thus, if the heater malfunctions, you will notice it during a daily check and before the water temperature is driven too high. If your aquarium does overheat in excess of 90°F, immediately remove 20% to 30% of the water and place floating ice bags in the aquarium. Save the water that you removed in buckets, let it cool, and return it when temperatures in the aquarium and in the buckets are similar.

Pollution

The least likely emergency situation is the sudden pollution of your aquarium. A dead fish left in an aquarium while the owners are away is typically responsible for this . In these cases, the water will be cloudy and smell unpleasant. You will need to conduct a 50% water change, change the filter carbon, and test the water. Change 20% more of the water if conditions do not improve. During this time, do not feed your fish until conditions in the aquarium have stabilized and returned to normal.

Part Four

Feeling Under
the Weather

Chapter 9

Keeping Healthy Clownfish

The first steps to keeping your clownfish healthy include providing a nutritional diet and clean aquarium water. However, your clownfish, like all marine tropical fishes, are subject to many kinds of maladies, which may be caused by pathogens in your aquarium. Fret not, you can greatly reduce the incidence of disease by reducing stress.

Stress and Clownfish

There are many ways to define the term "stress" and most of us think about the mental stress that we may encounter on a daily basis. When it comes to captive fish, like clownfish, stress refers to any condition where normal biological function is disrupted; in other words, stress occurs when something physical, biological, or psychological disrupts your clownfish. When this happens, your clownfish's resistance to disease is impaired and it may become ill. The best way, therefore, to avoid disease is to make life as stress-free as possible for your clownfish. You do this by avoiding stressful conditions.

Stressful Conditions

There are a number of physical and psychological sources of stress for your clownfish. By far, the most important is poor water quality. In the last chapter, we reviewed the basic maintenance routine for keeping your water healthy. In dirty water, your clownfish have to work harder to breathe, their heart rates increase, their internal balance is disrupted, and their own internal pH drops. In addition, their bodies react by producing a number of hormones that compromise the immune system. If the level of pollution is extreme, your fish will quickly die. Therefore, take the simple steps necessary to avoid poor water quality. Be sure to use water tests to diagnose water quality problems.

Every time that you chase your clownfish with a net, catch them, bag them, or remove them from the water, you are causing stress. Handling stress like this can cause death from respiratory failure, infections from physical damage, and immune system failure and disease. Your clownfish have a thick, protective mucous layer that acts as a first line of defense against infection and disease. When this layer is removed or damaged, harmful bacterial infection is possible. You can minimize handling stress by reducing the amount of chase and net time when you are moving a fish, keeping travel time short, and using a soft net that is large enough to accommodate the whole fish.

Overcrowding

Overcrowding your aquarium can have stressful consequences, because not having enough space leads to territorial disputes, fighting, and injuries. An overcrowded aquarium will eventually have poor water quality as well because too many animals create too much waste, which means pollution will occur.

Compatibility

Unfortunately, not all fishes will get along with your clownfish, and when this happens, you'll notice aggressive

The wide-band colwnfish (Amphiprion latezonatus) *is one clownfish species that does not flourish in a dynamic aquarium environment.*

behavior, which can involve fighting and injury. Injury, of course, can cause immediate death or lead to secondary infection and disease. Therefore, make every effort to choose fishes that get along with your clownfish.

Changes in Environment

Dramatic and sudden changes in temperature or specific gravity will create stressful conditions for your clownfish. If either rises or falls to levels outside the tolerance of your pets, the stress will kill them immediately. Even if the temperature or specific gravity remain within the tolerance level of the clownfish, a rapid change up or down can kill or weaken the fish, compromise the immune system, and lead to disease. Therefore, check your aquarium temperature and specific gravity routinely.

Any sudden change in light or sound can stress your clownfish. This includes tapping on the aquarium glass or switching the light on while the fish are resting. Once you establish a routine, your clownfish will adapt to it. Any sudden change will cause stress.

Diagnosing Problems

Before you can treat a problem with your clownfish, you need to be able to identify it. In general, the appearance and behavior of your clownfish will betray a problem. The sooner you notice stress, the faster you can address it. And, since you are feeding your fish twice a day, this is the best time for routine examinations.

If you notice a problem with one of your clownfish, see if the problem is affecting only one critter or the whole aquarium. If more than one fish is displaying symptoms of stress, your problem may be systemic, but if only one fish is affected, you may need to isolate it for treatment.

Physical Appearance

The most obvious indication of stress is the physical appearance of your clownfish. Physical characteristics that are indicative of stress or disease include discoloration, clouded eyes, frayed fins, and an abnormal stomach. These

Unlike the larger specimens, small clownfishes adapt more easily to aquarium life.

are the same factors that you consider when you buy a clownfish from your dealer.

Behavior

When you examine the behavior of your clownfish, remember that everything is relative when it comes to diagnosing your fish. It's the changes in behavior that count. Some species are naturally lethargic or prefer the safety of hiding places, and this may not be indicative of stress. The behavioral signs of stress include a noticeable lack of appetite, general laziness, gasping, and erratic swimming. One of the first signs of stress or illness is the loss of appetite. If you notice that one of your clownfish is not interested in food, offer it something that it normally cannot refuse, such as live food. A fish that becomes sedentary, lazy, or hides most of the time may be fighting some kind of ailment.

Erratic Swimming

If your clownfish is hyperventilating or gasping at the surface, this is a clear sign of stress, which may be associated with poor water quality and low dissolved oxygen. Erratic swimming, rubbing, or twitching behavior is clearly indicative of stress. It's not unusual for a clownfish infested with parasites to rub itself against the gravel and aquarium decorations.

Dealing With Stress

If any of these symptoms are manifesting themselves and you strongly suspect that one or several of your clownfish are suffering from stress or may have a disease, you need to act quickly. First, if the problem is with more than one fish, check for stressful conditions that are affecting the entire aquarium. Examine water quality, temperature, and specific gravity. Is the aquarium overcrowded? Has the aquarium routine been disrupted recently?

This skunk clown is exhibiting good color and a nice rounded appearance; both of these factors indicate that the fish is experiencing negligible amounts of stress.

On the other hand, if only one fish is showing signs of stress, then evaluate those conditions that may be specific to a single animal, like injury, handling stress, or disease. Once you have isolated a stressful condition, make every effort to stop it. If, however, you cannot attribute the problem to any particular cause, you will need to treat the ailment.

Chapter 10

Common Diseases
and Disorders

Even with your best intentions to keep your clownfish healthy by minimizing stress, a disease may slip by you and fall upon one of your pets. Nasty pathogens that cause disease are in and around your clownfish in the aquarium. They can be introduced with a new tankmate or in the water from another aquarium. These pathogens may be bacterial, viral, fungal, or parasitic. Some of the diseases caused by these agents will manifest themselves with symptoms that you can diagnose. Unfortunately, there are not a lot of treatments available for the home aquarist, and there are no guarantees that your clownfish will be saved.

Treatment Methods

Although the best remedy for disease in your aquarium is prevention, there are a few treatment methods you should be aware of in case your clownfish become ill. However, realize that despite all your efforts and the application of commercial remedies, the fish may still perish. Common treatment techniques include direct aquarium treatment with therapeutic agents, the hospital tank, the dip method, and internal medication. In all cases, don't hesitate to consult with a veterinarian who specializes in exotic pets and fishes.

You may be able to treat your clownfish with commercially available therapeutic agents added directly into your aquarium. Sometimes called the long bath, this method can be effective against some diseases, but not always. In some cases, the aquarium decorations or filter media may absorb these medications, or they may be toxic to filter bacteria. In almost all instances , fish medications are toxic to invertebrates. If your dealer recommends this treatment method, remove activated carbon from your filter because it will absorb many medications. If only one of your clownfishes is infected, it's best to isolate the fish in a hospital tank. As with all medications, follow the manufacturer's instructions closely.

The best hospital tank to use is a small aquarium (10 gallons or less). It typically has a sponge filter and good aeration, but no elaborate decorations and gravel. It's good to

This percula clown (Amphiprion percula) *is displaying some clamping of the fins. Clamped fins may indicate the start of a parasitic infestation.*

Excellent Aquariums start with TROPICAL FISH HOBBYIST

SAVE UP TO **63**%

provide some cover for the fish in the form of rocks or a flowerpot. You can isolate diseased individuals in a hospital tank for direct treatment without subjecting other fish to the treatment. The tank will also reduce the likelihood of the disease spreading to others in the aquarium.

The dip method involves removing the infected fish from the aquarium and dipping it into a bath containing a therapeutic agent or simply freshwater. The dip is brief enough not to injure the fish, but long enough to kill the pathogen. The freshwater dip involves dipping a fish infested with parasites into a freshwater bath for 3 to 15 minutes. The salt differences between the aquarium water and the treatment bath are enough to kill the pathogen rapidly without harming the fish.

Some remedies must be administered internally by injection or by feeding. It is not recommended that the average home aquarist inject clownfish. Feeding the fish medicated food is difficult because the correct dosage is difficult to estimate, the fish is not feeding normally, and you cannot guarantee that the fish being treated is getting the proper amount of food.

Common Remedies

The number of remedies for marine fish diseases available to the home aquarist is somewhat limited. Copper and antibiotics are the most commonly used, but their use can be risky and potentially harmful to your aquarium.

Copper

Although copper is a pollutant in the marine environment, it is considered by many to be a beneficial treatment for killing parasites. However, copper can adversely affect fishes, is not very stable in saltwater systems, and its fate in the aquarium is not fully understood. Some experts feel that copper should be eliminated as a treatment of aquarium fish diseases, but it is still widely used in the

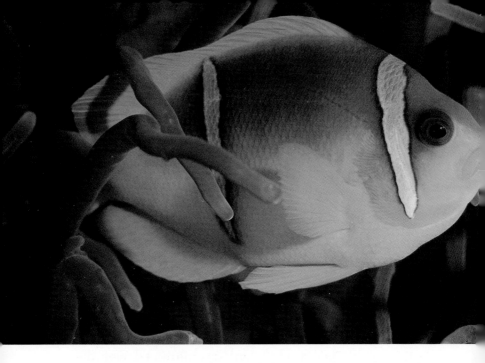

Captive-bred specimens of two-band clowns (Amphiprion bicinctus) *are not often available to hobbyists.*

aquarium trade. If you decide to use copper to treat your clownfish, it is suggested that you isolate the fish in a hospital tank for treatment. Also, copper is toxic to invertebrates, so do not administer copper in an aquarium with any kind of invertebrate.

Antibiotics

Antibiotics are therapeutic chemical agents that may be the most effective way of treating some of the common aquarium diseases. If possible, your clownfish should be treated in a hospital tank to avoid the effects of these compounds on an established aquarium.

Bacterial Infections

As you know, there are good bacteria and bad bacteria, and all of them are microscopic, single-celled organisms capable of very rapid reproduction.

Fin Rot

Symptoms: Erosion or rotting of the fins. In advanced stages, the disease spreads to the skin and gills, causing bleeding and ulceration.

Treatment: The incidence of this disease may reflect poor water quality. Improve water quality, remove uneaten food, conduct a partial water change, and change the activated carbon in your filter. The antibiotics furanace, augmentin, and ciprofloxin may be effective.

Fish Tuberculosis, Wasting Disease

Symptoms: External signs of this disease are often lacking until too late. In advanced stages, skin lesions, emaciation, labored breathing, scale loss, frayed fins, bulging eyes (popeye), and loss of appetite are signs of this infection.

Treatment: These bacteria are transmitted through raw infected fish flesh and the feces of infected fish; they can also infect skin wounds and lesions. Prevention is the best treatment; avoid feeding raw fish and shellfish to your aquarium occupants. If this disease heavily infects the aquarium, it must be sterilized and the water discarded.

Vibriosis, Ulcer Disease

Symptoms: Lethargy, darkening of color, anemia, ulcers on the skin and lower jaw, bleeding of the gills, skin, and intestinal tract, clouded eyes, loose scales, pale gills, and sudden death.

Treatment: These bacteria live in the intestinal tracts of healthy fish, but become dangerous when stress allows infection. Poor water quality, crowding, and excessive handling are common causes of stress. Immersion treatments with antibiotic compounds, including furanace, erythromycin, halquinol, and nitrofurazone have been successful.

Viral Disease

These simple microscopic organisms invade the cells of

their host and, in most cases, there are no treatments for the few viral diseases of the marine aquarium.

Cauliflower Disease, Lymphocystis

Symptoms: Fin and body lesions that are raised, whitish, warty, and have a lumpy texture like cauliflower. The lesions may take three to four weeks to reach their full size, and diseased fish will typically show few signs of distress, continuing to feed and behave normally. This infection is generally not fatal, but it can be transmitted to other fish in the tank.

Treatment: There is no effective treatment of this viral infection, but you should isolate the fish immediately and let the fish's immune system address it, which may take several months.

VEN, Viral Erythrocytic Necrosis

Symptoms: This virus attacks blood cells and exhibits no external signs on the infected clownfish. The infection is caused by significant stress, which weakens the fish's immune response.

Treatment: Stress prevention is the most effective treatment. Commercially prepared, immune system-boosting foods are good for suspected infections.

Fungal Disease

Fungi are plant-like organisms, some of which are parasitic on fishes.

Ichthyophonus Disease, Whirling Disease

Symptoms: Emaciation, spinal curvature, darkening or paling of the skin, roughening of the skin, fin erosion, skin ulcers, erratic swimming behavior, lethargy, and popeye. These fungi invade the internal organs of the fish, infecting the kidney, heart, spleen, and liver.

Treatment: Fungal cysts are usually ingested by the fish,

then burst and enter the fish's bloodstream and infect internal organs. Death results up to two months after infestation. Treatment is very difficult due to the internal nature of this disease, and the infected clownfish should be immediately removed from the aquarium to prevent other fishes from infection.

Exophiala Disease
Symptoms: Lethargy, disorientation, and abnormal swimming

Treatment: This is a poorly known fungus and no treatment is known. You should isolate the fish to prevent other aquarium fishes from infection.

Parasitic Infestations
Parasites range from tiny one-celled organisms called protozoa, to larger invertebrates like crustaceans and worms. It's not beneficial for the parasite to kill its host, but it can cause lesions that become secondarily infected by bacteria. Parasitic infestations can be internal or external.

Marine Velvet Disease
Symptoms: These parasites are too small to see, but the skin becomes dull, patchy, and velvet-like and white spots are visible on sections of intact skin. In advanced stages, the fish's behavior may include fasting, gasping, scratching against objects, and sluggishness. Lesions can lead to secondary bacterial infection.

Treatment: No completely effective treatment is known, although some antibiotics, including malachite green, nitrofurazone, and acriflavin are effective. The freshwater dip sometimes dislodges these parasites from the host, but does not kill them. Reducing the specific gravity of the aquarium to 1.011 for at least a month is needed to fully eradicate the infestation, but this should only be done if your aquarium contains only clownfish.

Marine White Spot, Cryptocaryoniasis, Saltwater or Marine Ich

Symptoms: Early signs include fasting, cloudy eyes, troubled breathing, excess skin mucus, and pale skin. In advanced stages, white spots appear on the skin, gills, and eyes and death follows within a few days.

Treatment: The white spot organism is very difficult to control and, like marine velvet, the encysted stage of this parasite is resistant to most treatments and remains in the gravel of the aquarium. The freshwater dip is effective at killing the parasites on the host but does little to treat the aquarium. Dropping the specific gravity to 1.011 for at least six days may treat the clownfish aquarium. Copper products and the antibiotic chloramin T seem to have limited effectiveness.

Percula clowns (Amphiprion percula) *are particularly sensitive to marine ich, so inspect your specimens closely and frequently.*

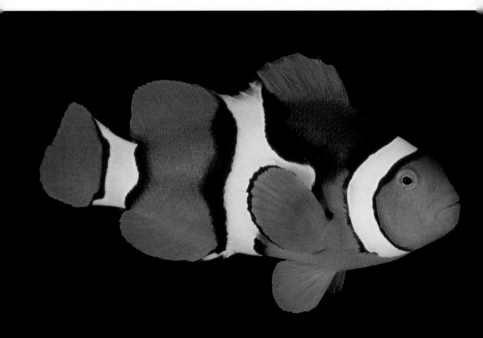

Brooklynella, Clownfish Disease

Symptoms: Thick, white mucus coat, rapid breathing, loss of appetite, and gasping. In advanced stages, fish have faded body coloration.

Treatment: To remove the parasites, use the freshwater dip and treat the aquarium with four drops of formalin per gallon of aquarium water. Formalin is toxic to invertebrates, so only use it in a fish-only tank.

Uronema Disease

Symptoms: External ulcers, muscle and skin bleeding, lethargic behavior, sloughing of the skin, and internal infection. Death may be rapid due to impaired circulation in the gills.

Treatment: There is no known treatment for this poorly known parasite.

Tang Turbellarian Disease, Black Spot

Symptoms: These flatworms look like numerous dark spots distributed unevenly over the fins, gills, and body. Other signs include fasting, listlessness, paling or whitish skin, and scratching against objects; secondary bacterial infections are known to occur.

Treatment: Flatworms are a type of parasitic worm that may be effectively treated with the freshwater dip and trichlorfon, and praziquantel immersion.

Trematode Infestations

Symptoms: These worms are so small that they cannot be seen with the naked eye. They infect the gills, eyes, skin, mouth, and anal opening. Infected fishes, which usually rub themselves against objects in the aquarium trying to dislodge the parasites, often develop a secondary bacterial infection.

Treatment: The life cycles of these animals are poorly understood, so it is difficult to treat this infestation. However, immersion in freshwater dip, mebendazole,

praziquantel, or trichlorfon has been effective. Preventative treatment includes the feeding of food mixed with metronidazole, piperazine, or praziquantel.

Crustacean Infestations

Symptoms: These tiny, crab-like organisms, called isopods, copepods, and argulids are visible to the naked eye. They feed by piercing the host and causing tissue damage. Fishes with heavy infestations swim erratically, rub against objects, and jump; bacteria infect lesions.

Treatment: Remove infested fishes immediately and treat them by immersing in freshwater, trichlorfon, malathion, or formalin baths. To kill egg masses, either dry aquarium decorations or immerse them in 2% bleach solution for two hours.

Other Health Problems

HLLE, Head, and Lateral Line Erosion

Symptoms: Holes develop and enlarge in the sensory pits of the head and down the lateral line on the body. The disease progresses slowly, but the fish does not behave differently and the disease is rarely fatal.

Treatment: This is a mysterious disease with no specific treatments, but some recommend the use of the freshwater antibiotic flagyl. Check your water quality and make necessary adjustments. Diversify your fish's diet and add vitamin supplements to its food.

Floating Bloat

Symptoms: The inability to descend to the bottom of the aquarium. Feeding clownfish floating pelleted food causes this temporary malady.

When treating parasitic infestations, be sure to remove all invertebrates from the aquarium.

Part Five

Advanced Clown Keeping

Chapter 11

Clownfish and the Reef Aquarium

With an aquarium full of healthy clownfish, it's only a matter of time before you venture into the realm of the advanced aquarist. Indeed, your clownfish represent the perfect starting point. You may start by adding an anemone to your tank, or perhaps some live rock, but make sure that your aquarium is prepared for such bold moves. Also, realize that this chapter is a good place to start, but I strongly urge you to read the more detailed references on this subject cited in the bibliography.

Getting More Sophisticated

The simplest and most popular type of saltwater setup is the fish-only aquarium, which is the concentration of most of this book. As implied by the name, the fish-only aquarium does not house invertebrates, which means that it is less expensive and requires less maintenance than the more complicated reef tanks that do house inverts. For many marine aquarists, a clownfish-only aquarium provides enough entertainment and represents an excellent balance of cost and benefit. For others, this is a starting point, and the desire to add more diversity to the tank becomes overwhelming.

The ultimate saltwater aquarium is called the reef aquarium, simply because efforts are taken to actually mimic the natural tropical reef ecosystem. This type of setup has also been referred to as the mixed species aquarium, the living reef aquarium, the mini-reef aquarium, the nano-reef aquarium, and the micro-reef aquarium. These aquaria include invertebrates like anemones, hard corals, shrimps, and snails, as well as a few peaceful species of fish. Your clownfish are perfectly compatible with these other inhabitants of the reef aquarium most of the time.

Before you decide to run out and buy a bunch of invertebrates and fish for your clownfish aquarium, there are a few things to consider. First, invertebrates are extremely sensitive to water quality and, therefore, require sophisticated filtration systems. Second, many fish species eat invertebrates, so you have to select your fish carefully. Third, many fish remedies will kill invertebrates, and you should be prepared to isolate ailing fishes.

Don't let these issues deter you from moving forward. Just be sure to bring your aquarium up to speed before investing money unwisely.

Special Needs

As I have already indicated, and I cannot emphasize this enough, invertebrates require excellent water quality in the aquarium. This means that you may have to beef up your filtration system and add other equipment, including a protein skimmer, specialized lighting, water movement, live rock, and calcium supplements.

In Chapter 2, we examined the types of filtration available to the home aquarist. If you intend to house invertebrates, I recommend that you choose one of the more sophisticated filtration systems, like the trickle filter (wet-dry filter) coupled with a protein skimmer. Highly advanced reef aquariums use the Berlin filtration system, which relies heavily on live rock and live sand. If you choose

This is a beautiful specimen of allard's clownfish
(Amphiprion allardi) *from Kenya, Africa.*

to keep your undergravel filter when you add invertebrates, you should augment it with a canister filter or an external power filter. Again, a protein skimmer would be mandatory in this case as well. Do not add invertebrates to an aquarium that relies solely on a sponge filter, as they would not likely live very long.

Intense lighting is critically important to invertebrates like corals and anemones that feed on the specialized algae (zooxanthellae) that actually live inside them. If these cnidarians are on your wish list, then actinic lighting should be on your equipment list. Actinic light bulbs produce light at the blue end of the color spectrum, which is ideal for corals and other photosynthetic invertebrates. However, actinic bulbs do not provide full spectrum light, so additional lighting will be needed. Actinic bulbs are produced for most of the lighting fixtures on the market today.

Quite a few of the popular invertebrate species, like stony corals, have calcium-based skeletons. To remain healthy, corals need a lot of calcium and the calcium level to remain stable, so you will need to maintain the carbonate hardness, or alkalinity, of your water. The first step, then, is to go out and purchase calcium and alkalinity test kits to measure both of these parameters. Next, supplement the calcium and balance the alkalinity by adding calcium hydroxide solution or kalkwasser (calcium water) to your aquarium on a routine basis. Kalkwasser will help maintain both calcium and alkalinity levels, but you may need to add calcium chloride to initially raise the calcium level.

Many advanced aquarium systems contain live rock, which is not actually rock that is alive, but rather rock that is alive with all kinds of tiny critters, including algae, shrimps, sponges, crabs, and worms. Live rock forms the basis for many reef aquariums because it provides biological filtration, decoration, and microorganisms for your clownfish to feed on.

Magnificent sea anemones (Heteractis magnifica) *are perhaps the most popular sea anemones kept for clowns.*

If you have ever snorkeled on a coral reef, you can't help but notice the movement of water around you. The health of the natural reef system is highly dependent on this water movement. In your reef aquarium, make sure to maintain high water currents, which will deliver food and remove wastes from your invertebrates.

Clownfish and Invertebrates

It would require an entire book to list all the invertebrate species that are compatible with clownfishes. In virtually every major group of invertebrates available to the average aquarist, there are members that get along fine with clownfish. It is probably easier to list those species that are poor tankmates than those that are compatible tankmates. Nonetheless, for those that are not familiar with the many invertebrate groups, the following is a brief overview of the most common. You will notice that each major group is referred to as a phylum, which includes families of species.

The most primitive invertebrates belong to the phylum Porifera, which we call the sponges. The bodies of sponges are organized around a system of water canals and chambers lined with hairs, called flagella, which move to create the flow of seawater through the sponge. Sponges typically exhibit bright colors of green, yellow, red, orange, or purple; they also come in a variety of interesting shapes, and they are well suited for the clownfish aquarium.

The phylum Cnidaria includes the jellyfish, hard and soft corals, sea anemones, sea whips, and sea fans. These are round-bodied invertebrates with a digestive cavity and a mouth surrounded by a circle of tentacles with stinging cells, which aid in the capture and ingestion of food. You are already familiar with the anemones, which, along with the corals, house photosynthetic algae in their bodies. Therefore, they require intense lighting as well as excellent filtration. Clownfishes live happily with many of the cnidarians available to the home aquarist, but they are especially partial to anemones. Thus, the most logical next step is to add an anemone to your aquarium after you make sure that your filtration is up to speed. Remember that clownfishes are pretty particular about their anemones, and of the 1,000 species of anemones, only 10 are natural hosts. Go back to Chapter 1 to review the anemones that are receptive to clownfishes.

The most familiar invertebrate group to most people is the phylum Mollusca, largely because many of us eat them. This group includes clams, oysters, scallops, mussels, squids, snails, and cephalopods. The mollusks have a body consisting of three major regions: a head with sense organs, a mouth, and a brain; a visceral mass surrounded by a body wall and containing most of the internal organs; and a foot, the muscular lower part of the body on which the animal creeps. In addition, the mollusks secrete a calcareous shell and possess a feeding organ called a radula. Some mollusks, like snails, thrive in the aquarium, while others, like many shellfish, are

This tomato clown (Amphiprion frenatus) *is enjoying the view from his anemone.*

difficult to feed. Clownfish get along with almost all of the mollusks, except the predatory squid and octopus, which are not recommended for the average reef aquarium.

The phylum Arthropoda is the largest group of animals on the planet, but most of these are insects. The marine members include the shrimps, crabs, and lobsters, which are characterized by a hard encasement called an exoskeleton. Clownfish get along fine with most shrimp and crabs in the reef aquarium, but be careful because smaller shrimp may be consumed and larger crabs may do the consuming. Lobsters are not recommended additions to the clownfish reef tank because they are boisterous and aggressive.

The invertebrates in the phylum Echinodermata are commonly known as starfish, sea urchins, brittle stars, sand dollars, sea cucumbers, and sea lilies. These critters have a unique water vascular system that operates numerous tiny tube feet that they use for locomotion and feeding. Some echinoderms, like starfish, have little suction cups at the end of the tube feet that help them cling to the substrate. With few exceptions, many of the echinoderms are compatible with the clowns.

Clownfish and Other Fishes

If you decide to add other fishes to your reef aquarium, your biggest concern will be choosing species of fish that are compatible with your invertebrates. Otherwise, clownfishes are generally compatible with most species of small fishes in the aquarium trade. Gobies, angelfishes, butterflyfishes, dragonets, surgeonfishes, tangs, blennies, grammas, and jawfishes are all suitable companions for clownfishes.

However, clownfish are bit territorial, like many members of the family Pomacentridae, but their bark is worse than their bite. Nonetheless, many of their closest relatives, the damselfishes, do not live comfortably with clownfishes. These two groups within the same family are highly territorial, which results in constant bickering and the

The longnosed hawkfish (Oxycirrhites typus) *is a great aquarium companion for all species of clownfishes.*

Here, an ocellaris clown (Amphiprion ocellaris) *is sharing his home with both a regal tang* (Paracanthurus hepatus) *and a coral beauty* (Centropyge bispinosa).

The miniata grouper (Cephalopholis miniata)
is a major predator of clownfishes.

all around disruption of the tank. Clownfish are also known to harass shy fishes like chromis and cardinalfishes, so it's best to keep these two groups apart.

On the other hand, larger predatory fishes like groupers, triggerfishes, lionfishes, snappers, and moray eels have been known to prey on clownfishes. In a well-fed aquarium, these predators are not likely to attack, but who wants to take the risk?

Chapter 12

Breeding and Reproduction

Advanced clownfish keeping doesn't have to include other fishes and invertebrates; it can start with just two clownfish with an attraction to each other. I have written repeatedly throughout this book that most clownfish in the aquarium trade are reared in captivity. Who's to say that you cannot rear your own? In fact, it is not unheard of for the average home aquarist to become a prolific clownfish breeder who actually sells young clownfish back to his dealer! This chapter represents a brief overview of clownfish breeding. If you are serious about breeding clownfish, I suggest that you consult with one of the more in-depth sources listed at the back of this book for additional information.

Clownfish Reproduction

You will recall from Chapter 1 that a sexually mature female and a sexually mature male dominate the social hierarchy of the clownfish. In a natural coral reef setting, these two fish will spawn twice a month for years, with the female depositing hundreds of eggs on a hard surface. The eggs, fertilized and tended by the male, will hatch after eight

This female saddleback clown (Amphiprion polymnus)
is guarding her batch of newly laid eggs.

days, and the tiny, translucent larvae will emerge and swim
to the surface, attracted by the moonlight. For the next one
to two weeks, the larvae, feeding on tiny planktonic animals,
will triple in size, develop into tiny clownfishes, settle to the
bottom, and seek a home in the tentacles of an anemone. If
the young clownfish finds an anemone, it will spend the rest
of its life there. If not, it will die in the mouth of a predator.

In a healthy, stable aquarium, your clownfish can be
induced to spawn naturally in captivity. If you can establish
the right conditions, or set the mood so to speak, your two
clownfish will spawn as they do in nature, with one
exception. On the natural reef, only a very small fraction of
young survives because they are preyed upon during all
phases of their development. On the other hand, you will be
able to control predation in your aquarium, so a very high
fraction of your baby clownfish will live, much higher than in
nature. Hence, your captive clownfish parents, or broodstock,
have a distinct advantage over their wild counterparts.

The Broodstock

Of the 28 species of clownfishes, 19 have been successfully reared in captivity. However, some species are easier to rear than others. While one clownfish may spawn readily, it may be more difficult to take care of their larvae and juveniles; this is the case with Clark's clownfish. On the other hand, the Percula clownfish is more difficult to spawn, but their larvae and juveniles are easier to rear. The easier species to start with include the Tomato, Red and Black, and Ocellaris.

The biology of the clownfish makes it simple to find a male and a female. As you know from Chapter 1, male clownfish readily change into females. Therefore, when you purchase a pair of clownfish, both will mature and one will become the female. If you want to tell them apart, the female is generally the larger and more dominant fish. In some species, like Clark's, there are color differences between males and females.

Well-conditioned maroon clownfish adults will readily spawn in many larger aquaria.

Sometimes, unusual color variations will result from captive-breeding projects. This is an example of the percula clownfish (Amphiprion percula).

Clownfish pairs will form naturally if they are in good health and not competing for space with a lot of other fishes. It's best to start with younger tank-reared fish when establishing your broodstock. The clownfish will compete with each other for dominance up to several months before a true pair bond is established. Once the hierarchy is set, the two clownfish will enter a courtship phase, remaining very close together as they bond. The spawning pair may take up to a year to fully establish a pair bond.

If you intend to spawn your clownfish, it is best to avoid having more than two in the aquarium. Additional clowns will increase the competition for dominance, thereby delaying the entire process. The breeding pair will also torment other clownfish.

Spawning

During the bonding stage, your clownfish will choose the optimal territory and spawning site in your aquarium. Before the pair is too far along, you must provide the right spawning substrate for the female's eggs. This is typically a hard material like a ceramic tile, clay pot, or rock pile. If you see your clownfish sharing a particular part of the tank, make sure there is suitable substrate nearby. The spawning site will become the fiercely defended territory and nest of the mating pair.

To initiate the spawning process, you have to provide your clownfish with a constant threat-free environment with stable water conditions, a regular light cycle, and dependable feedings. Frequent water testing, a light timer, and a consistent feeding pattern will increase the probability of spawning. When comfortable, the mating pair will initiate pre-spawning behavior, which includes aggression and erratic swimming. This behavior may last upwards of a month prior to their first spawn. About a week before actually spawning, the couple will clean a 2 to 5- inch space on the spawning substrate.

During spawning, the female lays her eggs on the substrate and the male fertilizes them over the course of one to three hours. The eggs, numbering about 400-1,500, remain attached to the substrate and are tended by the male while the female defends the territory. As the eggs develop, the color changes from bright orange to pink to gray by the sixth day. The eggs hatch on or about the eighth day at a water temperature of 80°F.

Taking Care of the Young

Adult clownfish and other tankmates will readily consume your newly hatched larvae. Therefore, it is very important that you establish a larval tank for the growth and development of your baby clowns. The larval tank is a relatively specialized setup that includes a 10-gallon tank with black shading on all sides (for the first six days) and no filtration, a heater (80°F), some aeration, and low lighting in 16-hour periods. Water for the larval tank should come from the broodstock tank immediately before transferring the eggs or larvae.

Small skunk clowns have a very broad stripe running down their dorsum. As they get older and larger, the stripe often becomes smaller.

To get your young clownfish to the larval tank, the substrate holding the eggs can be moved before hatching, or the larvae may be captured and moved with a light-colored bowl. Once in the larval tank, the yolk sac on the larvae will sustain them for about 72 hours, before they must be fed live foods for the next 10-12 days. For the first five days, the ideal food for larval clownfish is live rotifers in high densities three times per day. For the next three days, clownfish may be fed newly hatched brine shrimp and pulverized flake food thereafter.

Without a filtration system, your larval tank needs to be bottom cleaned with an aquarium vacuum twice a day. You do not need to change the water for the first two days, but you should change 20% for days three to seven and 10% for days eight to twelve. Your larval clownfish will metamorphose into baby clownfish during this latter period and then a sponge filter should be added to the tank.

This tomato clown has just outgrown his second band and is beginning to exhibit adult coloration.

The metamorphosis of larval clownfish into juveniles ranges from overnight to a couple of days depending on the species. The tiny clownfish less than 3/8" long will settle to the bottom of the tank. Pulverized dry foods, frozen brine shrimp, and live brine shrimp provide a suitable diet for the young clownfish. Juveniles can remain in the larval tank as long as a sponge filter has been provided or they can be transferred to a separate grow-out tank that is properly setup with an undergravel filter, heater, aeration, and light. After about six weeks, the light period can be reduced from 16 hours to 12 hours.

Juvenile fish can be transferred to the main aquarium as early as three weeks after hatching and as late as eight weeks, depending on how well they feed and the water quality in the larval tank. Young clownfish should be captured in a plastic container and transferred in groups.

Live Food

The survival of your larval and juvenile clownfish depends greatly on the quality of their food. In their natural environment, these young stages feed on live invertebrates like rotifers and shrimp. Unfortunately, there are no substitutes for this food in the aquarium, and you must provide this diet for your newly hatched and developing clownfish.

While live rotifers and brine shrimp are available from some specialized fish dealers, this is not always the case, and the average home aquarist must raise their own live foods. To do so typically involves rearing microalgae (tiny algae), rotifers, and brine shrimp at the same time. The microalgae are used to feed the rotifers and brine shrimp. While this process is not overly complicated, it is outside the scope of

This is a very uniquely colored ocellaris clown.

Clowns kept in large aquariums may not be able to compete for live foods unless they are delivered to the clowns individually.

this book. I recommend that any hobbyist who is seriously interested in rearing clownfish in captivity consult with the references in the back of this book for details on how to properly raise live foods.

Resources

ORGANIZATIONS

Federation of American Aquarium Societies (FAAS)
Secretary: Jane Benes
E-mail: Jbenes01@yahoo.com

Federation of British Aquatic Societies (FBAS)
Secretary: Vivienne Pearce
E-mail: Webmaster@fbas.co.uk

Marine Aquarium Council (MAC)
923 Nu'uanu Avenue
Honolulu, HI 96817
Telephone: (808) 550-8217
Fax: (808) 550-8317
E-mail: info@aquariumcouncil.org
http://www.aquariumcouncil.org

Marine Aquarium Societies of North America
Director of Membership/Secretary: Cheri Phillips
E-mail: cheri@uniquesensations.com
http://www.masna.org

The Breeder's Registry
5541 Columbia Drive North
Fresno, CA 93727
E-mail: tlang@aquariusaquarium.org
http://www.breeders-registry.gen.ca.us/index.htm

The International Federation of Online Clubs and Aquatic Societies (IFOCAS)
E-mail: ifocas@ifocas.fsworld.co.uk
http://www.ifocas.fsworld.co.uk

PUBLICATIONS

Tropical Fish Hobbyist
Tropical Fish Hobbyist magazine has been the source of accurate, up-to-the minute, fascinating information on every facet of the aquarium hobby including freshwater fish, aquatic plants, marine aquaria, mini-reefs, and ponds for over 50 years. TFH will take you to new heights with its informative articles and stunning photos. With thousands of fish, plants, and other underwater creatures available, the hobbyist needs levelheaded advice about their care, maintenance, and breeding. TFH authors have the knowledge and experience to help make your aquarium sensational.

Tropical Fish Hobbyist Magazine
T.F.H. Publications, Inc.
1 TFH Plaza
Third and Union Avenues
Neptune City, NJ 07753
Telephone: (800) 631-2188
E-mail: info@tfh.com
http://www.tfh.com

INTERNET

AquaLink
(http://www.aqualink.com)
The largest aquaria web resource in the world, AquaLink provides fishkeepers with information on a variety of topics, including freshwater and marine fish, aquatic plants, goldfish, reef systems, invertebrates, and corals.

Aquaria Central
(http://www.aquariacentral.com)
Aquaria Central is an online resource offering species profiles, help forums, chat rooms, and a variety of aquaria articles. To date, there are more than 700 species profiles listed on this website's searchable database.

Aquarium Hobbyist
(http://www.aquariumhobbyist.com)
This website lists upcoming marine-related events, as well as commercial pages, chat rooms, news, a classifieds section, and care information.

Reef Central

(http://www.reefcentral.com)
Reef Central is an online community that shares information regarding the marine and reef aquarium hobby. The site includes access to discussion forums, photo galleries, chat rooms, and news.

Reefs.Org

(http://www.reefs.org)
As an online interactive community, Reefs.Org is home to an active bulletin board, reference library, chat room, monthly periodical, and online curriculum.

Wet Web Media

(http://www.wetwebmedia.com)
This website features extensive aquarium, fish, and aquatic information, with numerous articles on marine aquariums, freshwater aquariums, aquarium plants, ponds, and other related topics.

VETERINARY RESOURCES

American Veterinary Medical Association (AVMA)

1931 North Meacham Road
Suite 100
Schaumburg, IL 60173
Telephone: (847) 925-8070
Fax: (847) 925-1329
E-mail: avmainfo@avma.org
http://www.avma.org

Bibliography

Burgess, W. E., H.R. Axelrod, and R.E. Hunziker III
Dr. Burgess's Atlas of Marine Aquarium Fishes
TFH Publications, Neptune City, NJ, 1990.

DeVito, Carlo and Gregory B. Skomal
The Everything Tropical Fish Book
Adams Media Corp., Holbrook, MA, 2000.

Fenner, Robert M.
The Conscientious Marine Aquarist
TFH/Microcosm Professional Series, Neptune City, NJ 07753.

Michael, Scott W.
*Reef Fishes; Volume 1: A Guide to Their Identification,
Behavior and Captive Care*
TFH/Microcosm Professional Series, Neptune City, NJ 07753.

Skomal, Gregory B.
*Setting Up a Saltwater Aquarium, An Owner's Guide to a
Happy Healthy Pet*
Howell Book House, New York, NY, 1997.

Skomal, Gregory B.
Saltwater Aquariums for Dummies
John Wiley and Sons, Hoboken, NJ, 2002.

Wilkerson, Joyce
*Clownfishes: A Guide to Their Captive Care,
Breeding & Natural History*
TFH/Microcosm Professional Series, Neptune City, NJ 07753.

Index

Photo Credits